BLUES
Rhythms You Can Use

A COMPLETE GUIDE TO LEARNING BLUES RHYTHM GUITAR STYLES

BY JOHN GANAPES

PLAYBACK+
Speed • Pitch • Balance • Loop

To access audio visit:
www.halleonard.com/mylibrary

Enter Code
8114-6593-3188-5357

ISBN 978-1-4234-5663-6

7777 W. BLUEMOUND RD. P.O. BOX 13819 MILWAUKEE, WI 53213

In Australia Contact:
Hal Leonard Australia Pty. Ltd.
4 Lentara Court
Cheltenham, Victoria, 3192 Australia
Email: ausadmin@halleonard.com.au

Visit Hal Leonard Online at
www.halleonard.com

ACKNOWLEDGMENTS

My thanks go to bassist Mike Derrick and drummer Randy Kramer for agreeing to play on the audio and helping to make the recording session a success—after only four days' notice and without any advance preparation. I'd also like to thank Curtis Blake for lending this project his prowess on the blues harp, and making it more fun and interesting for students of the blues.

Thanks also to Matthew Zimmerman of Wild Sound in Minneapolis for once again making the recording sessions relaxed and fun.

Thanks to all of my good friends at the Podium Guitar Shop in Minneapolis, for constantly creating a great place to hang out and be a player. And my thanks to Frank Spencer for loaning me his amp—it's a sweetheart.

Thanks to Jeff Schroedl at Hal Leonard for his calm and patience—especially with regard to deadlines.

And finally, as always, my love and gratitude go to my wife, Kathleen, and my girls, Alexandra and Sophia.

John Ganapes 2008
BluesYouCanUse.com

TABLE OF CONTENTS

		Page	Audio Track

How to Use This Book 6

Tuning Notes 1

Some Fundamentals
The notes, intervals, and how they fall on the fingerboard; building chords from the root up; chord types and their symbols; chord progressions and the I–IV–V 8

Lesson 1   **Basic Spread Rhythm**
Basic spread structure; two types of spread structure sets; eighth-note strums; fret-hand relief tricks 14
"Basic Spread" Full Band 16   2
"Basic Spread" Play-Along 16   3

Lesson 2   **Spread Along the Neck**
Adding the ♭7th to the spread structure; moving I, IV, and V along the neck; quarter-note triplets 18
"Spread Along the Neck" Full Band 20   4
"Spread Along the Neck" Play-Along 20   5

Lesson 3   **Spread for Mr. Reed**
Open-string spread; chord anticipation 21
"Spread for Mr. Reed" Full Band 23   6
"Spread for Mr. Reed" Play-Along 23   7

Lesson 4   **Plain Old Major Blues**
Major triads; fragments of larger chords; I–IV substitute; chord chops . . . 24
"Plain Old Major Blues" Full Band 27   8
"Plain Old Major Blues" Play-Along 27   9

Lesson 5   **Minor Triad Blues**
Minor triads and inversions; approach chords; dominant V chord in a minor key; single note/chord combinations; shifting chord shapes 28
"Minor Triad Blues" Full Band 31   10
"Minor Triad Blues" Play-Along 31   11

Lesson 6   **Simple Seventh Chord Rhythm**
Dominant seventh chords; passing chords; precise strumming 32
"Simple Seventh Chord Rhythm" Full Band 35   12
"Simple Seventh Chord Rhythm" Play-Along. 35   13

Lesson 7   **Funky Blues**
Building chords above and below the root; sixteenth-note rhythm 36
"Funky Blues" Full Band 38   14
"Funky Blues" Play-Along 38   15

Lesson 8   **Ninth Chord Rhythm in A**
Ninth chords; Set 1 ninth chords; ninth chord approaches; ninth chord chops 39
"Ninth Chord Rhythm in A" Full Band 41   16
"Ninth Chord Rhythm in A" Play-Along 41   17

Lesson 9   **High Nines in D**
Set 1 and 2 ninth chords; ♭II chord; quarter-note and
eighth-note-triplet combos 43
"High Nines in D" Full Band 46   18
"High Nines in D" Play-Along 46   19

Lesson 10   **Sixes and Nines**
Chord fragments; ninth-to-sixth chord movement; multi-stop slide;
simplification for learning 47
"Sixes and Nines" Full Band 50   20
"Sixes and Nines" Play-Along 50   21

Lesson 11   **Ninth Chord Study in E♭**
Treble string ninth chords; elongated ninth-to-sixth chord slides 53
"Ninth Chord Study in E♭" Full Band 56   22
"Ninth Chord Study in E♭" Play-Along 56   23

Lesson 12   **G Minor Blues**
Building minor seventh chords; dominant V chord in minor keys;
dotted-sixteenth-note rhythms 57
"G Minor Blues" Full Band 60   24
"G Minor Blues" Play-Along 60   25

Lesson 13   **D Minor Blues**
Set 1 and 2 minor seventh chords; minor ninth chords; arpeggios 61
"D Minor Blues" Full Band 64   26
"D Minor Blues" Play-Along 64   27

Lesson 14   **Got the Drive**
Minor i–IV substitute; chords derived from the Dorian mode;
minor-major chords; use of thumb in chords 65
"Got the Drive" Full Band 67   28
"Got the Drive" Play-Along 67   29

Lesson 15   **Passing Chord Rhythm in A**
Thirteenth chords; seventh sharp nine chords;
diminished seventh chords; simplification for easier learning 69
"Passing Chord Rhythm in A" Full Band 73   30
"Passing Chord Rhythm in A" Play-Along 73   31

Lesson 16   **Triplet Stormy Rhythm**
Secondary chords; triplet strumming 74
"Triplet Stormy Rhythm" Full Band 76   32
"Triplet Stormy Rhythm" Play-Along 76   33

Lesson 17   **Jump Blues in A♭**
Interchanging dominant chords; syncopation 78
"Jump Blues in A♭" Full Band 80   34
"Jump Blues in A♭" Play-Along 80   35

Lesson 18   **Rockin' Boogie in A**
Major chord shapes; rhythm riffs; swing eighth-note strum;
rests and syncopated pushes 82
"Rockin' Boogie in A" Full Band 84   36
"Rockin' Boogie in A" Play-Along 84   37

Lesson 19 **Lead Rhythm in C**
Lead riffs in rhythm part; chord and pentatonic scale relationships;
fret-hand position 85
"Lead Rhythm in C" Full Band 87   38
"Lead Rhythm in C" Play-Along 87   39

Lesson 20 **Rockin' Blues for Jimi**
More seventh sharp nine chords; sharp ninth to thirteenth
chord movement; shapes common to I–IV–V chords 88
"Rockin' Blues for Jimi" Full Band 91   40
"Rockin' Blues for Jimi" Play-Along 91   41

Lesson 21 **Dominant Rhythm in G**
Partial seventh and ninth chord voicings; active melodic rhythms 92
"Dominant Rhythm in G" 95   42

Where to Go from Here 96

All music composed and arranged by John Ganapes.
Produced by John Ganapes.
Recorded at Wild Sound Studio, Minneapolis, MN.
Engineer: Matthew Zimmerman.

Musicians:
John Ganapes—Guitars
Mike Derrick—Electric Bass
Randy Kramer—Drums

with special guest:
Curtis Blake—Harmonica
(Courtesy of Blue Bayou Records)

HOW TO USE THIS BOOK

Who Can Use This Book

This book was designed for you if:

- You have finished *Blues You Can Use* or beyond (*More Blues You Can Use* and *Jazzin' the Blues*).

- You are at an intermediate guitar level and can play chords with reasonable comfort.

- You know some blues chords and progressions, but just don't know what to do with them (strumming, arpeggios, etc.).

- You want to be able to accompany singers and soloists, or play rhythm when it's not your turn to solo at a jam session.

- You teach guitar and need an organized approach to blues-rhythm guitar styles and techniques.

- You want to start or join a blues band and you realize that you will be called upon to play rhythm more often than lead.

Level of Study

This book begins at an intermediate level and quickly moves all the way to advanced rhythm guitar techniques. If you have worked through much of *Blues You Can Use*, you are ready to begin this book.

The theory given in this book is very brief and intended primarily for review. It is not necessary to understand music theory in order to use and benefit from this book. While it is a great help and can really expand your musical horizons, you do not need to know theory to play the blues.

(Rather than repeating some material already fully covered in other books in this series, that information is referenced in this text including specific page numbers.)

How Much Time to Spend on Each Lesson

This is a very personal matter and depends entirely on your level of experience, knowledge of chords and progressions, technical ability (strumming and fingering chords, etc.), how many days a week you can practice, and how much each day.

You should take your time with each lesson, sticking with it until you are comfortable enough to move on. If you are having problems with a particular lesson and you really can't stand to practice it any more for the moment, or you are not making any progress after two or more weeks, put it aside and move on with the idea that you will come back to it a little later. It's amazing how sometimes after leaving a lesson on the back burner for a while, you can play it perfectly—or much better anyway—when you come back to it.

You should try to master the chords and techniques in each lesson before moving too much further along.

Audio Supplement

The *Blues Rhythms You Can Use* audio contains all of the studies in the book. The recording has drums and bass along with either a guitar or harmonica solo, so you can experience how it is to accompany an actual soloist.

Each study is given twice. The first is with the rhythm guitar featured prominently along with the bass, drums, and soloist. The second time, the rhythm guitar part is absent, so you can be the rhythm player.

Each study begins with a one-measure count off before the tune starts.

 The first track has tuning notes.

TRACK 1

What Else Do I Need to Know and Where Can I Find it?

Visit **BluesYouCanUse.com** and **JohnGanapes.com** on the web. There you'll find supplements, explanations, fingerings, and all sorts of information that will help you with this and many other aspects of your playing. There is always new information being added. If you don't find what you need right away, you can come back later and find it, or you can ask the author through the forum (free to join!). Here, the members from around the world discuss their studies in the *Blues You Can Use* series, their favorite players, equipment, and much more. You can also hear music recorded by the author and forum members.

SOME FUNDAMENTALS

Before you get started in this book, there are a few elements of harmonic theory that you need to know. They will be presented here, but very briefly; not much is explained in depth. If the following information is entirely new to you, or it just doesn't make sense, there are two options that I see for you:

The first is to ignore the theory entirely, or at least the parts you don't understand, and move on to the rhythm studies themselves. You can do that and you will still be able to play and learn the styles, chords, and techniques presented in this book and you will be fine. You don't have to know theory to play the blues. You'll just have to skip the discussions on harmony and focus on the music itself.

The second option, which I find to be more appealing and useful, is to use the references I give you throughout the book, and study the theory further. For the most part, I will be referring to the *Blues You Can Use Guitar Chords*, but I also make references to *Blues You Can Use* (the first book and "flagship" of the series), as well as, *More Blues You Can Use*, and even *Jazzin' the Blues*.

I believe that the more theory you know, the better off you will be and the more "places you can go" in whatever style of music you choose. It won't hurt your playing at all—that is simply a myth.

The Notes, Intervals, and How They Fall on the Fingerboard

It's important to know the notes on the fingerboard even if you play entirely by ear. You have to be able to find an A♭7th chord if required, or tell somebody, "play a C♯ note at the end of this lick," etc. You need to know where the D notes fall on the fingerboard in order to play a D minor pentatonic or blues scale.

The best way I know to learn them is by doing. For example, find all of the E notes on the bottom two strings, in order to find all of the possible 6th- and 5th-string-root E9 chords. Or, find a C on the 4th string and play a one-octave C major scale—that type of thing. I think it's much better than drilling yourself on the notes of the fingerboard. It's not that there is anything wrong with drilling yourself. I did my fair share of it, and you may need to do some, too, but learning by doing seems to work better in most cases, because you are not only learning the notes but also how to finger the chord or scale in question as well.

You have to have a reference to begin, so here is a chart of the notes on the fingerboard:

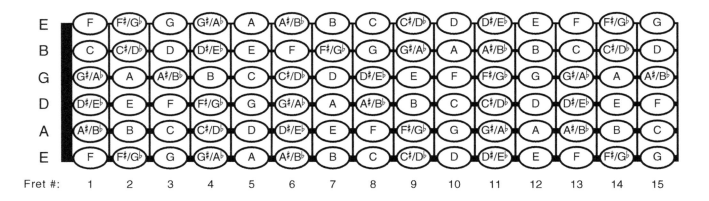

Building Chords from the Root Up

In Western harmony, chords are built using *every other note of a scale*. We will use the diatonic major scale—the "do-re-mi" scale you probably sang in grade school. Diatonic means seven-note, so it is a seven-note scale which repeats for an octave or more. As an example, the C major scale consists of the notes C–D–E–F–G–A–B (no sharps or flats). Continuing on in the second octave, you begin with a C an octave higher and move through the notes again. Here it is on the guitar:

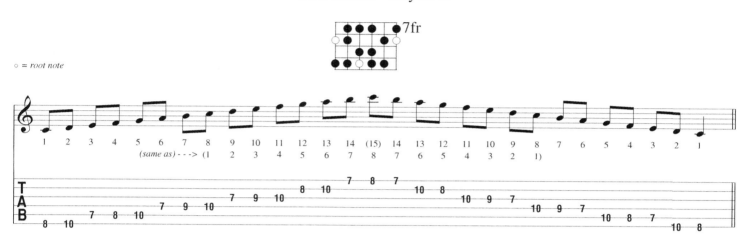

Diatonic Major Scale

Two Octave - Key of C

○ = root note

Using the above C scale, we can make any type of C chord, from major and minor triads (three-note chords) to sevenths, ninths, elevenths and thirteenths. We can alter any of the notes by sharping or flatting it (except for the root) to result in a different chord type.

Remember, we use every other note of the scale starting on the root note. Since we are using the C major scale, the root note will be C. Skipping the next note (D, or 2nd of the scale) we reach the 3rd (E). Then we skip the 4th step (F) and come to the 5th (G). We give the notes of the chord the same number they have in the scale, so C–E–G are the root, 3rd, and 5th, respectively.

It is major because the 3rd of the chord (E) is from the major scale. If we want to make the chord minor, we have to lower (flat) the 3rd by a half step, making it an E♭.

Going back to the C major triad, we can make it a C7 chord by adding the 7th step (B) and flatting it. The dominant seventh chord has a flatted 7th, so adding a B♭ to the C major triad results in a C7 chord. The notes of the chord are now C–E–G–B♭ for the root, 3rd, 5th, and ♭7th.

If you want to make a Cm7 (Cminor7) chord you have to flat the 3rd of the dominant chord like you did with the triads. The notes are C–E♭–G–B♭ for the root, ♭3rd, 5th, and ♭7th.

You can then add extensions to the seventh chords to create ninth, eleventh, and thirteenth chords. As you may have guessed, this involves selecting the 9th of the scale (D) to make a C9, the 11th (F) to make a C11, or the 13th (A) to make a C13.

You can omit some notes in these voicings to make a better sounding chord or more manageable fingerings on the guitar. Those abbreviated chord voicings are pointed out throughout the book.

All of the previous information is explained thoroughly in *Blues You Can Use Guitar Chords*. Here's what it all looks like:

Building Chords from a Major Scale

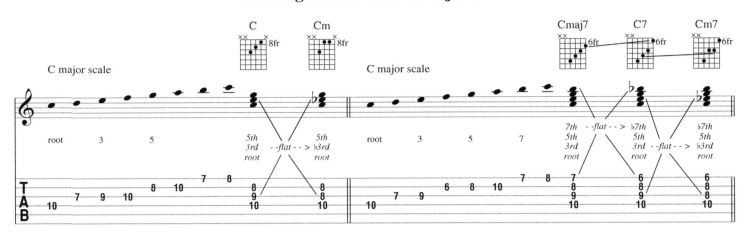

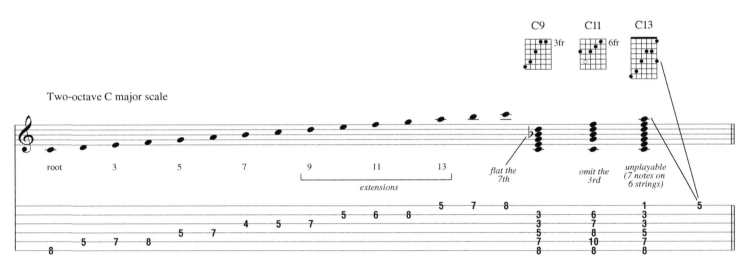

That was an extremely brief explanation, and as such, it is not intended to be anything more than a review. If this is all new to you, go to *Blues You Can Use Guitar Chords*—a companion book in the currently five-book *Blues You Can Use* series. In it you will find an in-depth explanation of chord construction and function, with lots of different chord voicings all over the guitar.

Chord Types and Their Symbols

You saw some of the chord types above; now, we'll set out a full list of the basic types.

Triads are the smallest and most fundamental chord type. They are three-note chords and are the building blocks for the rest of the larger chords. There are four basic triads: *major, minor, diminished,* and *augmented*. They look like this:

The Four Triad Types

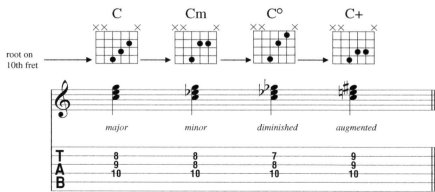

Next come the seventh chords. These are considered "complete chords" because even if you add any extensions to them, their basic type and function doesn't change. While there are four types of triads, there are only three types of seventh chords: *major, minor,* and *dominant.* You can add the 7th to a diminished or augmented triad, but they also fit into minor and dominant categories, respectively. Here they all are:

Seventh Chord Types

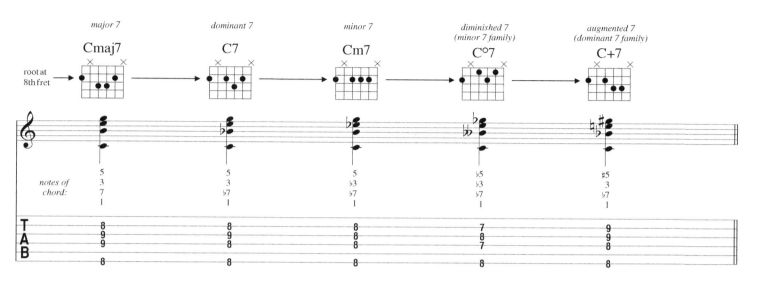

As I stated above, if you add an extension (9th, 11th, or 13th) to a seventh chord, it will still be either major, minor, or dominant, depending on the seventh-chord type you started with. That's why they are interchangeable—theoretically.

While there is no absolute and universal set of chord symbols, these are some common ones that are widely used:

Chord Type	Symbol	With C Root
major triad	(letter name of chord), M, Maj	C, CM, CMaj
minor triad	m, min, "-"	Cm, Cmin, C-
diminished triad	dim, "o"	Cdim, C°
augmented triad	aug, "+"	Caug, C+
major seventh	M7, Maj7, Δ7	CM7, CMaj7, CΔ7
dominant seventh	7	C7
minor seventh	m7, min7, -7	Cm7, Cmin7, C-7
diminished seventh	dim7, °7	Cdim7, C°7
augmented seventh	aug7, +7, 7♯5	Caug7, C+7, C7♯5

All extensions have the same symbols as the seventh chord you start with.

Here they are:

major seventh base	M9, Maj9, Δ9
	M13, Maj13, Δ13
	(Note: there is no major 11th chord)
minor seventh base	m9, min9, -9
	m11, min11, -11
	m13, min13, -13
dominant seventh base	9, 11, 13
augmented seventh base	aug9, +9, 9♯5
	(Note: the ♯5 and 11th clash and aren't used together. The same is true with the ♯5 and 13th.)

(Note: there are other chord types not listed here which can be found in *Blues You Can Use Guitar Chords, More Blues You Can Use,* and *Jazzin' the Blues.*)

Chord Progressions and the I–IV–V

A *chord progression* is the sequence of chords in a tune. Most often in the blues, the chord progression follows the *12-bar blues form.*

As its name suggests, a *12-bar blues form* is 12 measures long (a bar is the same as a measure) and is divided into three four-bar phrases or sections. Each four-bar phrase is a line in the verses of the tune. It works as follows:

phrase 1:	*statement*	"Nobody loves me and I'm really feeling down"
phrase 2:	*repeat statement*	"Nobody loves me and I'm really feeling down"
phrase 3:	*finish statement*	"If my baby won't love me, you know I'll leave this town"

Almost all blues songs fall into this category.

The most basic 12-bar blues progression is the I–IV–V progression. In it, you use only three chords: the I chord, IV chord and V chord of the key you are in. They change with every key, but their relationship to each other remains the same. The I, IV, and V chords are called the *primary chords* of the key. These are built on the 1st scale step (root), 4th scale step, and 5th scale step of whatever key you are in. If you are in the key of G, that is your I chord, the IV is C, and the V chord would be D. We almost always use at least a seventh chord, if not a ninth or thirteenth, so they would be G7, C7 and D7. As their names indicate, they are dominant-seventh chords.

The actual chord progression is as follows:

phrase 1:	‖ I | I |	I | I |
phrase 2:	| IV | IV |	I | I |
phrase 3:	| V | IV |	I | V ‖

Another 12-bar progression, the *quick-change progression,* is commonly used. It is called *quick change* because you change to the IV chord in measure 2, to break up the four solid measures of the I chord. The rest of the progression is identical to the basic progression. Here it is:

phrase 1:	‖ I | IV |	I | I |
phrase 2:	| IV | IV |	I | I |
phrase 3:	| V | IV |	I | V ‖

The last two measures of the tune constitute what is called the *turnaround*. Very simply, it is where you "turn around the tune" to the I chord at the top of the 12-bar progression. Usually, the turnaround moves from the I chord in measure 11, to the V chord in measure 12. The V chord "wants" to move to the I chord because there is a strong tendency for the V–I movement.

There are other basic chords in a blues key built on the remaining scale steps. These are called *secondary chords* and are ii, iii, and vi, built on the 2nd, 3rd, and 6th notes of the scale. In the key of G, they are Dm7, Em7, and Am7. You can see these are all minor chords, which is why we use lower case roman numerals for their names.

There is also the ♭VII chord, built on the flatted 7th step of the scale. In G, it is an F7 chord. It is used less often than any of the others.

Here's what they all look like in relation to the G major scale:

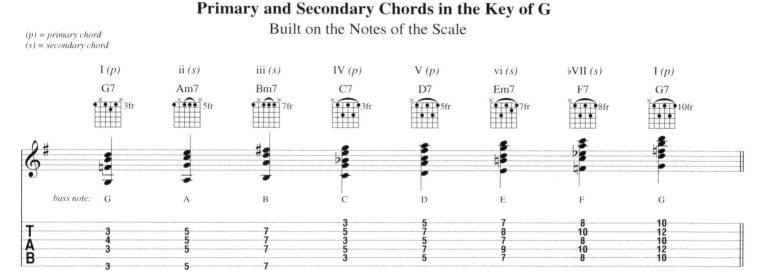

Primary and Secondary Chords in the Key of G
Built on the Notes of the Scale

(p) = primary chord
(s) = secondary chord

Throughout this book, you'll learn how and where to use primary and secondary chords in a 12-bar blues progression. You can find a full listing of all the keys on pages 115–116 of *Blues You Can Use Guitar Chords*, and pages 75–76 of *Blues You Can Use*.

BASIC SPREAD RHYTHM

The best place to begin your blues rhythm guitar study, I think, is with *spread rhythms*. These rhythm patterns are very common and easily recognizable. Everybody has heard them in both blues and rock settings. They get their name from the fact that your fingers are "spread" along the fingerboard as you play them. Because you strum on every eighth note, you can create a full and driving accompaniment for singers or soloists, or an unaccompanied rhythmic tune.

One note: for readers who feel that the spread rhythm studies are too simple and elementary, be sure to take a little time to look at them. There are three in this and the next two chapters, so play through them at least once to be sure that there isn't something you don't already know. Also, at least skim through the text because there may be some point of theory, technique, or hints that will be helpful to you. If after that you find it is still too basic, move on to the next lessons. Remember, this book is laid out progressively—each rhythm adding on to the previous ones—so even the early studies have information that is useful for anyone, including professionals.

THE CHORDS (HARMONY):

Basic Spread Structure

While there are many ways to vary it, a basic spread rhythm is played on two adjacent strings simultaneously (harmonically), creating a shape which is a sort of two-note chord, except that, as you'll recall, *a chord is made up of three or more notes*. The bass note (bottom note) is most often the root of whatever chord you are on in the progression. For example, if you are playing over an A chord, you will have an A note in the bass. The top note of the basic spread shape is the 5th of the chord (an E note in this case), found on the next string up and two frets up. If you are on a D chord, you start with a D in the bass, and the 5th of the chord, (A), would be two frets up on the next string.

Two Types of Spread Structure Sets

There are two common sets of I–IV–V chord-spread shape sets. The first has the root of the I chord on the 6th string and is referred to as a *6th-string-root chord*. The roots of the IV and V chords are found on the 5th string and are called *5th-string-root chords*. I call it *Set 1* of the I–IV–V chords. The second set, which I call *Set 2*, has a *5th-string-root I chord*, with the roots of the IV and V found on the 6th string. In either set, the two-note shape of the V chord is two frets up from the IV-chord shape (whether they are on the 5th or 6th string). These are introduced in *Blues You Can Use*, pp. 21–23.

The top note alternates between the 5th and 6th of the chord. The 6th of a chord is two frets above the 5th on the same string.

Since you play the spread rhythm on the bottom strings, you end up playing the bottom two strings of a barred 7th chord. The diagrams on the following page illustrate what they look like on the fingerboard.

Movable I–IV–V Spread Structures

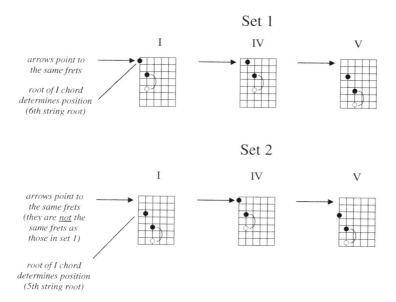

The above spread shapes are moveable, so they may be played up and down the fingerboard while staying the same distance from each other. Notice the arrow on the left side of the diagrams—it is always pointing to the same fret, even when the actual shape or chord is located on another fret. For example, in the key of A, the arrow points to the 5th fret where the I and IV chords are located, but the V chord is found at the 7th fret. This is the same standard on page 11 of *Blues You Can Use*.

On a very important note, the Set 1 and Set 2 shapes are NOT located in the same position. You find them by locating the position of the chord's root—usually the I chord. So, if you are in the key of G, the 6th-string-root shape of the I chord (Set 1) is found at the 3rd fret. Still in G, the 5th-string root shape of the I chord (Set 2) is found at the 10th fret. Some students get confused over this with disastrous results, so be careful. If you are at all unsure as to how this works, look again at the above illustration.

This rhythm study is a two-chorus tune where you play through the progression twice. In this case, *chorus* means one time through the entire 12-bar form. The first chorus has Set 1 spread shapes with a 6th-string-root I chord, and 5th-string-root IV and V chords. The second chorus has Set 2 spread shapes with a 5th-string-root I chord, and the IV and V are 6th-string-root chords.

THE STRUMS (RHYTHM AND TECHNIQUE):

Eighth-Note Strums

As I pointed out in the beginning of this chapter, in a spread rhythm, you almost always strum on every *eighth note* (eight strums for one bar of 4/4 time). The count/strums are "1-and, 2-and, 3-and, 4-and," using downstrokes almost exclusively. While it's a very simple rhythm, you create a full, and, at faster tempos, driving sound with it. When there is no bass player, you can use a basic spread to help fill in the bottom register. This works quite well in that situation.

Be sure to use the fingerings given in the following score and use only downstrokes with your picking hand.

BASIC SPREAD

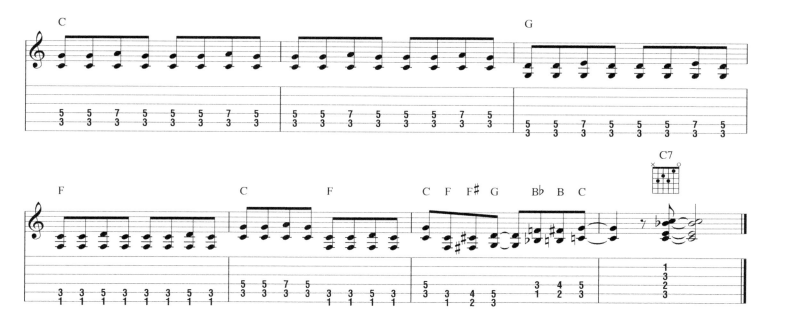

I wrote the above rhythm in the key of C, because it is easier to play the spread pattern there. The frets are narrower and closer together so you don't have to spread your fingers too far, and at the same time, they are wide enough to easily fit your fingers there. As you become comfortable with the spread, try moving the shape down the neck, one fret at a time, until you reach the 3rd fret where the frets are wider. Finally, move down to F at the first fret where it is the most difficult to play. Work your way down slowly.

Fret-Hand Relief Tricks

The spread rhythm can be quite a workout for your hands, so be sure to rest them frequently and shake out your fretting hand to relax it. I used to play with the late Mississippi bluesman Percy Strother, who would call as many as five spread tunes in a row. My left hand would get stiff and tired, and begin to cramp, so I learned a few ways to ease the strain. One is to take your thumb off the neck and lightly pull back with your whole arm to fret the notes. Also, fretting the 6th of the chord with your 4th finger creates most of the strain, so for two or three measures I would omit that note and just play the root and 5th combination. Sometimes I would do that for a whole chorus if my hand was cramping badly enough! It works pretty well and sounds fine for a short stretch.

The other thing I learned was that if I move up the neck to the IV and V chords instead of playing them on the next strings up, I would be in the area where it's easier to play, like I mentioned above. Little things like that are what can keep you going through a night of playing. The study in the next lesson illustrates the last technique, as well as position playing.

SPREAD ALONG THE NECK

The basic spread-rhythm style and technique was pretty thoroughly introduced in the first lesson. In this lesson, we'll see another way to move between the I, IV, and V chords—along the neck, as opposed to the *position playing* we did in the first study.

We'll also learn another note you can use in the spread pattern, in addition to the root, 5th, and 6th of the chord we have been using. It will allow you to play a bigger, bluesier chord.

Finally, we'll alter the rhythm in a couple of places in the progression—just to change things up and make it more interesting.

THE CHORDS (HARMONY):

Adding the ♭7th to the Spread Structure

This rhythm uses the same two-note shape we learned in the last chapter, but now we add another note to the shape: the ♭7th. This new note comes from the dominant seventh chord, and is found one fret above the 6th we have been using so far. So now we alternate between the 5th, 6th, and ♭7th on the top note of the pattern. It looks like this:

Spread Structures with ♭7th

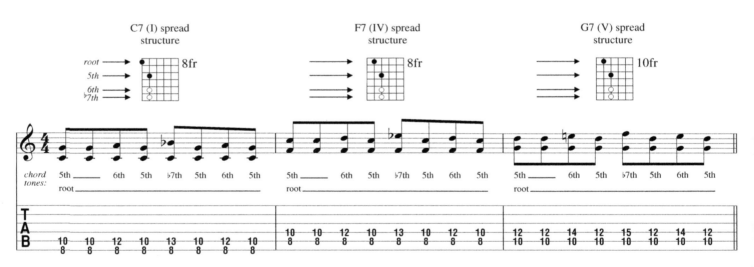

Because the ♭7th comes from the seventh chord, the spread pattern suggests a dominant harmony. That is, it gives us the dominant seventh chord sound, though it is spread over a beat-and-a-half before we hear all the notes.

Try playing the above shapes in a 12-bar blues progression. To begin with, play it in C, which is the key of the above example, because it is easier to play further up the neck. All you do is plug in the shape for the I, IV, or V chord where you see it indicated in the progression in the "Chord Progressions and the I–IV–V" section of the "Some Fundamentals" chapter. You can use the basic 12-bar progression or the quick-change progression found there.

THE STRUMS (RHYTHM AND TECHNIQUE):

Adding the ♭7th requires a wider finger spread (between the 1st and 4th), so it puts more strain on your fretting hand. Be careful not to overdo it. Give yourself a break by sometimes skipping the ♭7th and use the methods I gave you to help avoid strain and cramping. Also, when you're practicing, take frequent breaks or go on to some other element of your practice routine that doesn't put strain on your hand. It takes time to strengthen and limber your fretting hand enough to handle a long stretch of spread-rhythm playing.

Moving I, IV, and V Along the Neck

One new technique is moving along the neck to play chords using 6th-string root spread shapes. Instead of using the root-movement patterns from the last study, you move up five frets from the I to the IV chord. To find the V chord, move up seven frets from the I, or, as always, up two frets from the IV chord. In the key of G, you find the root of the I chord on the 6th string, 3rd fret. Instead of playing the IV chord on the next string up like the previous studies, move up five frets on the 6th string to the 8th fret (C). The root of the V chord is found two frets up from there at the 10th fret. While we move along the 6th string in this study, you can do the same using 5th-string-root spread shapes.

Moving I–IV–V Spread Structures Along the Neck
6th-String Root

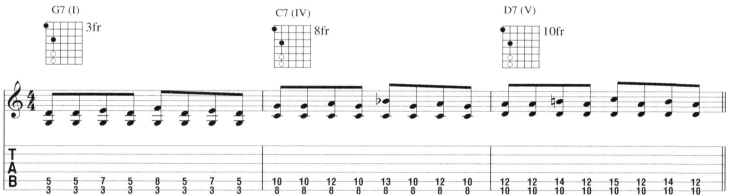

5th-String Root

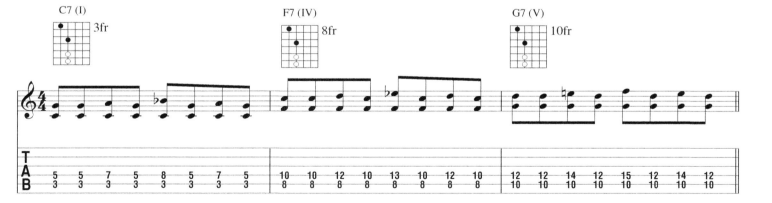

The strumming is the same as the first two rhythms, using downstrokes exclusively. Be careful to strum only the two bottom strings. Try not to sound the adjacent strings. This is a bit tricky at first, so be patient and practice it slowly at first. Listen carefully to what you are playing and correct any unwanted notes produced by hitting other strings.

You may notice in the following study that where there are two bars of a single chord, the $\flat$7th is omitted in the second bar. That is not only for variety but also to save your hand for those four short beats. That can make a big difference in the amount of strain you encounter—especially when the tune is extended, with lots of vocal verses or solos. Also, the study doesn't have the $\flat$7th on the G shape at the 3rd fret, because down in the lower positions the frets are wider and playing the wide spread puts even more strain on your hand.

Quarter-Note Triplets

Watch the *quarter-note triplets* (three notes in the space of two beats) in measure 4. They are used to walk up the neck from I chord (G) to the IV (C). Rather than try to analyze them, just listen to how they sound and play them by feel. That's the surest way to get them right.

SPREAD ALONG THE NECK

TRACK 4
Full Band

TRACK 5
Play-Along

LESSON 3

SPREAD FOR MR. REED

No study of spread rhythms would be complete without looking at those made famous by the great Jimmy Reed, who gave us such classic tunes as "Bright Lights, Big City," "Big Boss Man," "Honest I Do," and many more.

Along with his high-pitched, wailing voice, and his even higher-pitched, hauntingly eerie *blues harp* (harmonica), Reed found new variations of the spread to offer us. He often favored playing the two-note shapes one note at a time, or melodically, giving a different feel to the rhythm.

This rhythm study is in that melodic spread style, as heard in his tune, "Baby What You Want Me to Do."

THE CHORDS (HARMONY):

Open-String Spread

The shapes used here are the same as in the last rhythm, but because the tune is in the key of E, we use open strings for the roots of the I and IV chords on the 6th and 5th strings, respectively. This gives you a big, ringing sound that you can't get anywhere other than on open strings. Here are the open-string root spread shapes for A, D, and E, which constitute the I, IV, and V chords of the key of A, respectively. Try playing a spread rhythm in A to get a feel for the open-string shapes and an idea of their sound.

Open Root, I, IV, and V Spread Shapes in the Key of A

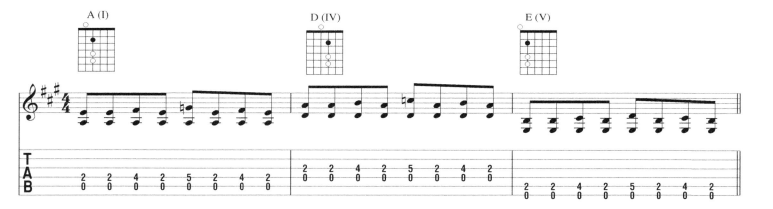

Once again, we add the ♭7th of the chord to the spread shapes. For the I and IV chords this is easy, because of the open-string—there is no stretch. The ♭7th is not added to the V chord, because the 2nd-position shape is more difficult to play due to wider frets.

This is a quick-change progression like the previous two studies.

THE STRUMS (RHYTHM AND TECHNIQUE):

Chord Anticipation

With this spread, you play the bottom note (root) of the shape on the upbeat, and the top note (5th, 6th, or ♭7th) on the downbeat. In order for this to work out with the root sounding first, you have to pluck it on the upbeat of beat 4 in the previous measure. In the beginning of the tune, you use a half-beat pickup playing the root of the I chord. Then you play the 5th on the downbeat of the first full measure. In other words, you are anticipating the chord change by a half beat. It might be easier to see in this diagram. This technique is sometimes called *pushing*, as in "push the chord change" (play it an eighth note ahead of the downbeat).

Push (Anticipation) in a Spread Rhythm

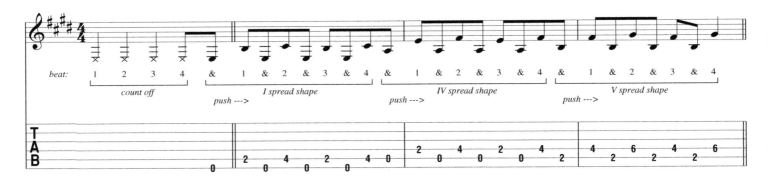

On the following page is the study itself. The eighth-note pushes are marked in the score. You'll no doubt feel how using open strings takes all of the strain off your fretting hand.

Use all downstrokes and be careful to only strum the notes indicated in the score. Listen closely for unwanted notes.

SPREAD FOR MR. REED

TRACK 6
Full Band

TRACK 7
Play-Along

Key of E

PLAIN OLD MAJOR BLUES

Now we will move away from the two-note spread structures and turn our attention to complete three-note-chord types. The first of these is the major triad discussed in the chapter titled "Some Fundamentals," found at the beginning of the book.

In the blues, we almost always use seventh or extended chords (9ths, 11ths, and 13ths), while we sometimes use major or minor triads. That being the case, the logical place to begin studying their use is with major triads.

We won't be satisfied with simply strumming the chords, so we'll use a common device in the blues and R&B styles—the I–IV substitute—to add interest to the chord progression.

THE CHORDS (HARMONY):

Major Triads

With the two-string spread shapes we studied earlier, only the root and 5th of the chord forms the foundation of the structure. On the top, we alternate between the 6th and the ♭7th (that replace the 5th), but none of the notes include the 3rd of the chord—an essential note in determining its quality (major, minor, dominant, etc.). With a spread rhythm, we let the notes of the melody and any other chordal instruments, if present, determine that. With the presence of complete chords, triads, or larger, any ambiguity disappears.

There are many, many possible voicings of major triads—far too many to list them all in this book (you can get an extensive listing of them in "Section 2: Chords" of *Blues You Can Use Guitar Chords*, beginning on page 44). We'll use only a few here. They are in the following diagram.

Chords Used in "Plain Old Major Blues"

○ = root note (not all double roots are marked)

With some chords, not all of the notes are used. The brackets below indicate which strings are used in those chord fragments.

Fragments of Larger Chords

You will notice that we don't always use the entire chord voicing, especially where notes are doubled. Instead, we get the sound we want from a smaller part of the voicing, though they contain the three notes of the triad. The fragments of the larger chord shapes are marked in the diagram. Using the smaller shapes give us not only a unique sound, but they are easier to finger, enabling us to nimbly and fluidly play more complicated chordal passages.

I–IV Substitute

Because the triads are rather plain sounding compared to sevenths and the extended chords, we need to do something to add interest to the progression. In this study, we do this with what is called the *I–IV substitute*. That is where, just for a brief moment, you think of the chord you are on as the I chord—no matter what key you are in—and move to its IV chord and back again. It doesn't really count as a chord change, but it gives you a little of the *I'm a Man* sound that Muddy Waters so ably perfected. You can use this for any major chord where you have enough time. If you are in the key of G and you change to the IV chord (C), you can play C–F–C which is I–IV–I in the key of C; you were thinking, just for that bar or two, in the key of C. Similarly, if you change to a D chord (V in the key of G), you can play a D–G–D or I–IV–I in the key of D. It works for any major chord, but it works a little differently with minor chords.

Here's what some of them look like in the key of G:

I–IV Substitutes

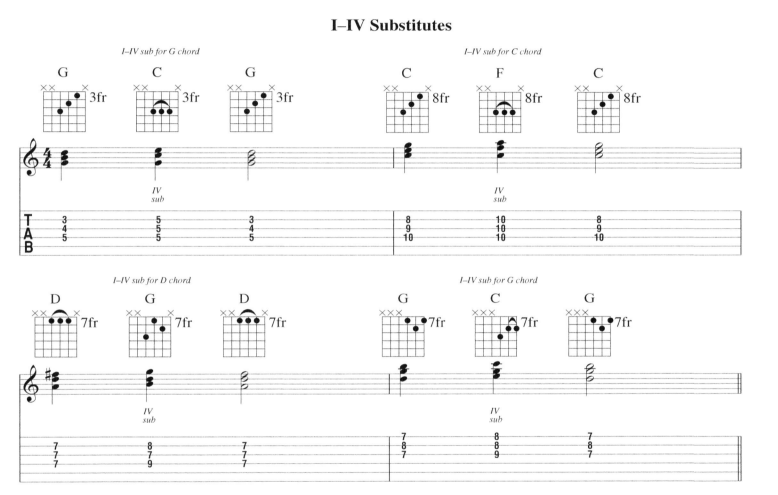

The important thing to remember here is that *the substitute is related to the chord and not the key*. Some chord substitutes will result in a chord that is not found in the key you are in, or it has a different quality than it normally would be in that key. They are marked in the rhythm-study score.

THE STRUMS (RHYTHM AND TECHNIQUE):

The strumming of this tune requires tighter pick control where you only strum three or four strings instead of all of them. Use all downstrokes.

Another challenge may be the quick moves up and down the neck required to make the chord changes on time. Use a nice, light touch, and try to achieve a smooth, gliding motion as you move along the fingerboard. If you press too hard, you will have a stiff feel and won't be able to make the position changes with the ease of a light touch.

For those who need some extra practice fingering the I–IV chord substitutes, I have included the following exercise. This will help you make the I–IV changes, develop more control of your picking, and acquire the lighter touch mentioned above. While you practice this exercise, be sure to take it slow enough to maintain control for clean and steady playing. Watch and listen for all of the elements you are trying to strengthen.

I–IV Substitute Exercise

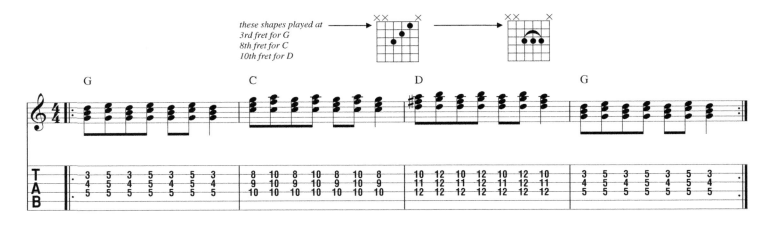

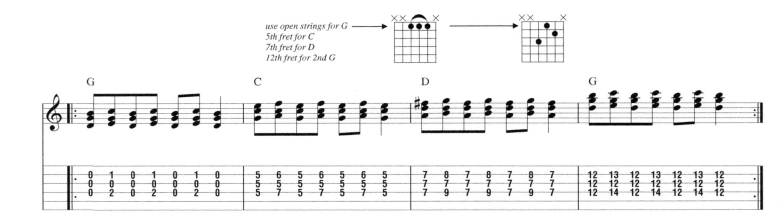

Chord Chops

One more thing to consider is the *chord chops*, where you cut the chord short, or "chop it." You do this by letting up on your fretting fingers very slightly—just enough to mute the strings. The chops are indicated in the score by a *staccato mark* (dot over the notes). Look for them and try to execute it.

All of the above techniques, and those which are given later in the book, are what make your playing more musical. If, however, you are not quite at the level of proficiency to be able to perform them and still keep the tune going, drop them. The primary goal is to make the chord changes on time and keep the beat. If you find that enough to work on, then cut out the refinements like chops, hammer-ons, and the like. You can always go back later and put them in, but it does no good to develop them at the expense of a steady, even beat. Learn the basics first then, if needed, the refinements later.

PLAIN OLD MAJOR BLUES

Key of G

LESSON 5

MINOR TRIAD BLUES

In the last lesson, we saw how we can use simple major triads in a blues setting. In this lesson, we'll do the same with minor triads. This time, instead of making use of any chord substitution devices, we'll make use of different inversions of the minor triads and *approach chords* to add interest.

Minor chords and keys can be very beautiful and moving. Most people respond to a minor blues very positively. They seem to touch something deep inside most of us. You can be quite expressive and often find that ideas flow of their own accord. The rhythm guitar parts are no exception.

In this lesson's study, you will move around the fingerboard a fair amount, so you have to keep in mind the light touch introduced in the last lesson.

THE CHORDS (HARMONY):

Minor Triads and Inversions

The opening chord is a G minor triad (Gm), almost identical to the opening major triad in the last study. It's in the same position with almost all the same notes and fingerings with one exception—the 3rd of the chord is flatted (lowered one half-step or fret). It's the note on the 3rd string and is what makes the chord minor as you saw in the "Some Fundamentals" section of this book.

The chord voicing is in root-position where the *tonic note* (root) is in the bass, or bottom note. Following immediately is the first inversion of that chord, which means that the 3rd is now in the bass, but all of the notes of the chord are still there in a different order. Here are the chords with inversions, as well as the minor barre chords introduced in the study:

Chords Used in "Minor Triad Blues"

Minor i, iv, v

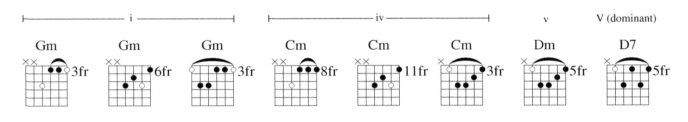

○ = *root note (not all double roots are marked)*

Approach Chords

Actually, the first inversion Gm chord is preceded by an F♯m triad, which is the same shape as the Gm, but is one fret below. It is called an *approach chord* and moves up to the Gm, first inversion chord. It is an *approach chord*, because it is how you get to the *target chord* (Gm), and doesn't count as a chord change.

You can use an approach chord almost anywhere there is time to play it. All you do is, fret the same shape as the target chord below or above (usually one fret away), and move to the actual chord of the progression. If you listen to the rhythm guitar part of blues recordings—and you really need to be doing just that—you will hear approach chords being used all the time.

Dominant V Chord in a Minor Key

You will notice that the v (Dm) chord in measure 9 is a minor triad, but there is a V7 (D7) chord in the turnaround. In a minor key it should be minor, but changing the v chord to a dominant chord makes for a stronger ending and is a technique that has been used for hundreds of years. It should stand out to your ear, because it makes the listener take notice that something important is happening in the music—in this case, we are "turning around" to the top of the tune for another verse.

In the second ending, we have a Dm chord and, in the second half of the measure, we change it to a D7. This is an even more dramatic change and is used to signal the tune's ending.

THE STRUMS (RHYTHM AND TECHNIQUE):

Single Note/Chord Combinations

The chord shapes used in this tune are not difficult to finger, but there are some tricky elements to the rhythm part:

First, the combination of single-note lines and chords is a challenge that takes a little practice. The reason for this is that your fretting hand is in somewhat different positions for each technique. You have to accurately pick the single-note lines, and strum three, four, or more strings for the chordal parts. You have to adjust accordingly and very quickly. If you worked through *Blues You Can Use*, you'll remember that the first two lead guitar studies presented this same challenge. Keep your fretting-hand wrist as straight as possible, while staying relaxed. Work through it slowly and you shouldn't have any serious problems.

Shifting Chord Shapes

The other problematic elements are the shifts between inversions and the use of approach chords. You have to see the target chords—the i (Gm) and iv (Cm) chords—and then fret the exact same shape a half-step lower to get to the approach chord. Then, you slide up to the target chord. When you slide from one chord to the next, be sure to press as lightly as possible. If you use a light touch, you will be able to develop a smooth glide between the chords. A heavy, hard touch will cause you to stick on the fret and produce a rough, uneven slide. This technique holds true for single-note slides as well. The following exercise will help you to perfect the sliding technique.

Exercise in Sliding into Chords

○ = *notes of approach*
chord in diagrams

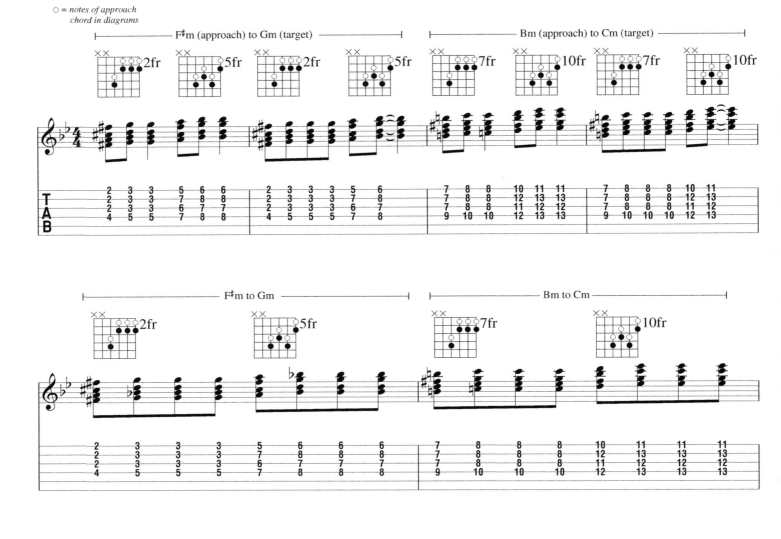

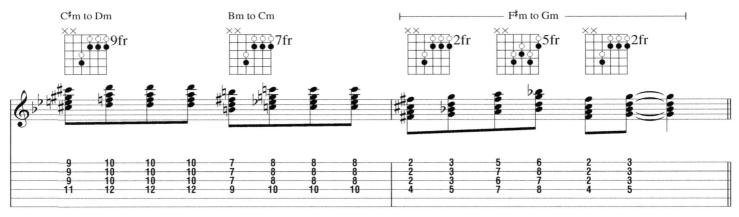

Watch for the staccato marks and give the chords a little chop where indicated. Remember to use a light touch on the slides! That is so important that it bears repeating.

TRACK 10
Full Band

TRACK 11
Play-Along

MINOR TRIAD BLUES

Key of G minor

LESSON 6

SIMPLE SEVENTH CHORD RHYTHM

At this point, we're ready to move on to fuller and bluesier chords: *seventh chords*. They are fuller because they have four unique notes instead of the three notes of the triad; they're bluesier because the extra note—the ♭7th—is one of the "blue notes." They have an edge that you don't get with a major or minor triad, and that creates the tension that characterizes the blues.

You will learn how to strum small segments of a larger chord. While you hold a larger four-, five-, or six-string chord, you will only strum a few of the strings—sometimes only one note.

We'll also continue with the use of approach chords, and see how to use "double" approach chords that are commonly used in the blues.

THE CHORDS (HARMONY):

Seventh chords, as you saw in the "Some Fundamentals" section of this book, contain a triad with an added 7th. (Look back there if you don't remember exactly how that works, or look in *Blues You Can Use Guitar Chords* for a more in-depth explanation.) You'll also recall that there are three basic qualities of seventh chords: major, minor, and dominant. While there are a few other types, they fit into one of the above categories. In the blues, we really only use the minor and dominant seventh chords. In this rhythm study, we'll focus on the dominant sevenths.

Dominant Seventh Chords

Dominant sevenths are created by adding a ♭7th to a major triad. They are the foundation of all dominant type chords and give the blues its harmonic sound and character. The ♭7th is found ten frets up from the root of the chord, or, if you invert it, two frets below the root. Here's how you make some major chords into dominant sevenths:

Making a Dominant Seventh Chord from a Major Triad

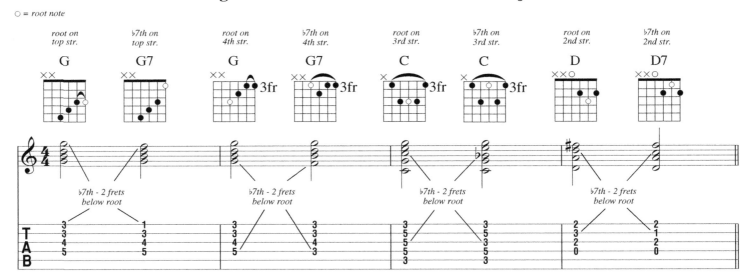

We'll use a few different voicings of the I (G7), IV (C7), and V (D7) chords in the key of G. They are all from the basic 6th-string-root and 5th-string-root barre chords. Here they are (Notice that the C7 chords are from the same basic 5th-string-root chord, though the 2nd form does not include the root.):

Chords Used in "Simple Seventh Chord Rhythm"

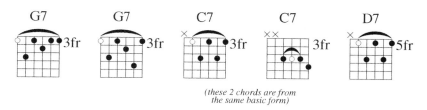

(these 2 chords are from the same basic form)

○ = *root note (not all doubled roots are marked)*

Passing Chords

The approach chords are not given above, though they are marked in the score. There is a passing chord in measure 9 (the D♭7), which "passes" between the D7 (V) and C7 (IV) chords. It works the same as approach chords, but moves between two chords of the key instead of up or down to a single target chord. (These are explained more thoroughly on pages 58 and 59 of *Blues You Can Use*.)

THE STRUMS (RHYTHM AND TECHNIQUE):

Precise Strumming

As I mentioned before, you will need to use a tighter strum, because you don't necessarily play all of the strings covered by the chords. For example, the G7 chord in the first full measure has only the bottom four strings sounding, even though you hold the full six-string voicing. Next, you pluck the bass note, which is also the root of the chord, and follow with strums of the top five strings while you continue holding down the root. You can see that this is all right-hand strumming (sorry lefties) technique. You don't change your fretting hand at all. When you use this type of strumming technique, don't worry about sounding a precise set of strings. You might get the bottom three or four strings on one stroke, and on the next, only the bottom two or three—that's okay because you get the fundamental sound (bassy, lower strings in this case). You just want to get the lowest or highest string you are thinking of to sound. Following is an exercise to help you get started with this selective-strumming technique—try making up some of your own, or just "doodle" with it.

Exercise in Strumming Segments of Larger Chords

Note: use all downstrokes

Move this shape up from 3rd to 10th position as indicated ------------>

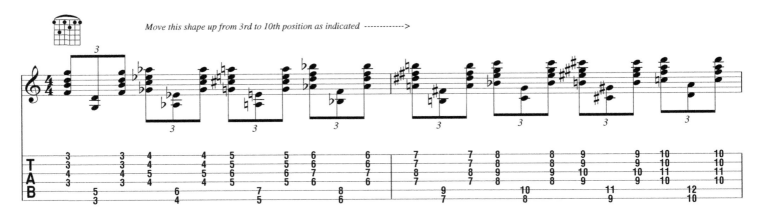

Move this shape down from 10th to 3rd position as indicated ------------>

G7

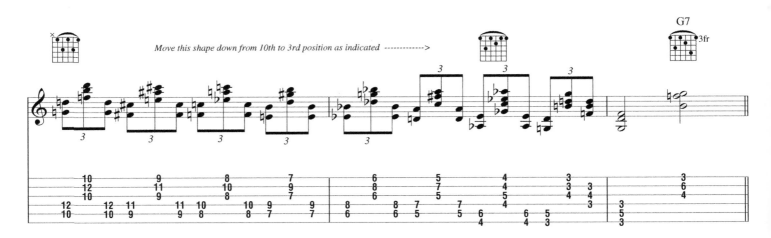

Note: after playing the exercise as written, work them in the opposite direction—1st exercise down the neck and the 2nd one up.

You'll find that as you get more accomplished with this technique, you will be able to get many different sounds out of a single, unchanging voicing. On the next page it is used in an actual tune.

SIMPLE SEVENTH CHORD RHYTHM

* = approach chord

**passing chord

LESSON 7

FUNKY BLUES

The study for this lesson has a common funky rhythm to it where there is a lot of syncopation. This gives the tune drive and, at the same time, a sort of "bumpy ride" feel. You will get a good workout in your strumming hand using both up and down strokes to produce this effect.

You'll also learn a new seventh-chord voicing—one that complements the ones you have already learned.

THE CHORDS (HARMONY):

Among the chords are the 6th-string-root voicings you used in the last rhythm study, with the addition of a different type of 5th-string-root voicing. The new voicing is built down the neck from the root, instead of above the root, like we have seen so far.

Building Chords Above and Below the Root

It is important to know that you can build a chord above the root (up the neck) or below it (down the neck). This is all on the same root in the same position. We have already built sevenths above roots on both the 6th and 5th strings. (Note: above or up the neck means towards the bridge or body of the guitar; below or down the neck, of course, means toward the nut or headstock.) When you build above the root, it simply means that the notes of the chord are either found at the same fret as the root or above them. As an example, look at the B♭7 chord in measure 2. It has a 6th-string root at fret 6 and the remaining chord tones lie on the 6th fret, or on the 7th and 8th frets.

Now look at the first chord in the tune (F7). It has a 5th-string root, but the rest of the notes are either found at the same fret as the root or below it, on the 6th and 7th frets. Look at the following diagram to make things clear:

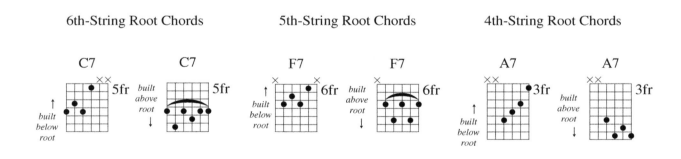

You can build scales in basically the same way, except that you have a third choice in some scales, where they are built in-between those found above and below the root. But that, while interesting and important, is beyond the scope of this book.

THE STRUMS (RHYTHM AND TECHNIQUE):

Sixteenth-Note Rhythm

The strums in this study are what really give it its character. You need to follow the strum-direction marks (downstrokes and upstrokes) carefully. The principle used in determining which to use is simple. The tune has a sixteenth-note rhythm, meaning that each beat is divided into four equal sub-beats. Those sub-beats are often counted like this:

1 - e - & - a, 2 - e - & - a, 3 - e - & - a, 4 - e - & - a

The numbers (1, 2, 3, and 4) are downbeats and they are played with downstrokes. The "&" (and) is a sort of secondary downbeat in a sixteenth-note rhythm, so they are played with downstrokes. The "e" and "a" are upbeats, and are played with upstrokes.

This may seem a bit confusing at first, but just try playing the first measure over and over without changing chords. Do this until you have it down, then move on to the B♭7 chord in measure 2 and do the same thing. Continue until you feel comfortable with the rhythm.

When you are playing a complex rhythm like this one, it is absolutely essential for you to keep track of where the downbeats are—remember, that's where the numbers are in the beat, so you have to know where beats 1, 2, 3, and 4 fall in the measure. To help you with this, they are marked in the score. Note that some of the downbeats are found on a rest (silence) or a tied note, where you only continue to let the chord ring without strumming again. You still want to feel the downbeat—usually it is best to mark it by tapping your foot or nodding your head, or some other physical act. Take your time with this one.

FUNKY BLUES

 = downstroke

V = upstroke

Key of F

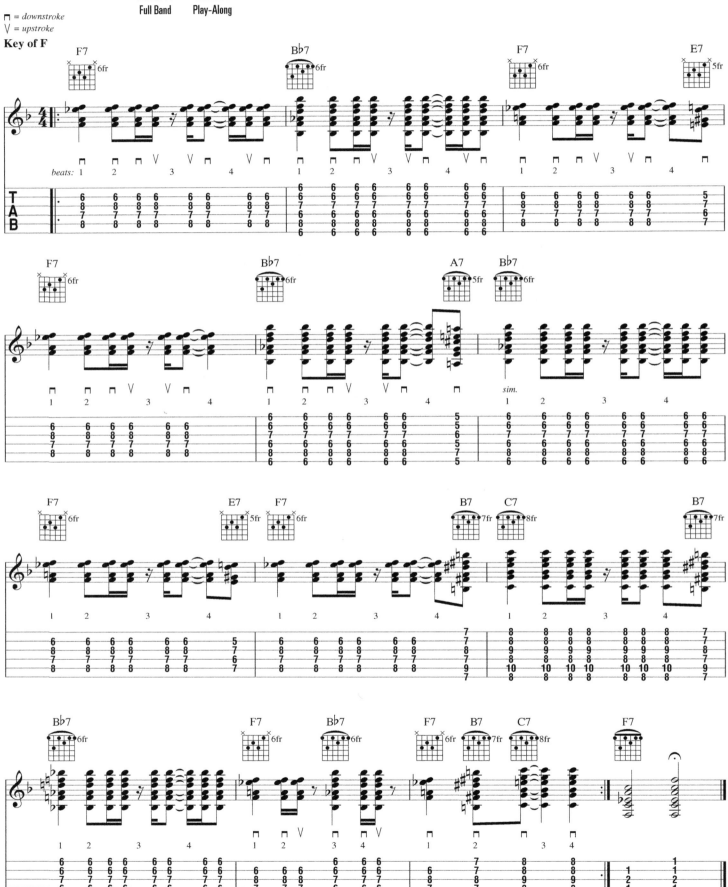

NINTH CHORD RHYTHM IN A

In this lesson, we'll introduce a new type of chord into our repertoire—the *ninth chord*. It is a more sophisticated sounding chord, compared to a plain seventh chord, that gives you a smoother and more modern sound.

We'll see how to move between the I, IV, and V chords using approaches that slide into the target chords from above and below. You'll hear a sound that is familiar to anybody who listens to the blues. Ninths and sevenths are the bedrock of blues harmony.

THE CHORDS (HARMONY):

Ninth Chords

Like the seventh chords we have already been using, a ninth chord is a dominant chord type. And like the seventh chords, you can alter them to make major and minor ninth chords.

Like the seventh chords, if you only have the chord name followed by a "9" (e.g., A9, B♭9), it is understood to be a dominant chord. So, if you see a chord labeled A9, you will know it is a dominant chord and is compatible and interchangeable with A7.

You saw in the "Some Fundamentals" section that full ninth chords are five-note chords made up of a seventh chord (root, 3rd, 5th, and ♭7th) with a 9th added on top of the stack. Since the seventh chord is the fullest chord you can make using every other note of a one-octave scale, you have to go into the second octave to find the 9th. It is the first of the extensions found in western harmony.

All ninth chords have a seventh chord contained within them. For that reason, ninth and seventh chords are interchangeable. That is, they are *theoretically* interchangeable. Sometimes a ninth just doesn't sound right where a seventh chord does, or a ninth chord sounds good while a seventh does not—you have to rely on your ear as the final judge.

Set 1 Ninth Chords

The ninth chords used in this study are Set 1 chords, where the I chord has a 6th-string root and the IV and V chords have 5th-string roots. There is also a 5th-string-root I chord at the end of the tune. You will notice that the 6th-string root of the first I chord is not played: it is omitted! You still have to look for the root on the 6th string in order to find the chord. This is the same Set 1, I–IV–V root-movement pattern you saw used with the spread shapes in Lesson 1.

Ninth Chord Approaches

The primary chords of the key (I, IV, and V, or, A9, D9, and E9) are reached via approach chords. Remember that approach chords are not part of the key and don't count as chord changes, but only move to the target chords which are part of the key. You saw how that works with seventh chords, but it also works well with ninths—maybe even better. There are also *double approaches* (two chords moving to the target from two frets away). You can see an example of this at the end of measure 8 where D9 and D♯9 move up to the E9 target chord.

Here are the ninth chords used in this study:

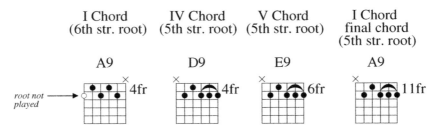

Note: only the I, IV, and V chords are included (not the approach chords).

THE STRUMS (RHYTHM AND TECHNIQUE):

Ninth Chord Chops

This study is very rhythmically simple. The strumming is pretty straightforward and easy. You have to watch for the punctuating chops (marked by the staccato dots in the score) that give the rhythm much of its character.

This exercise is designed to help you get comfortable with using ninth chord shapes, and the staccato chop. Take it slow and steady. You can stay on one chord for as long as you need to, lengthening the whole exercise.

Some of the staccato marks are labeled in the exercise to be sure that you recognize them.

Ninth Chord "Chop" Exercise

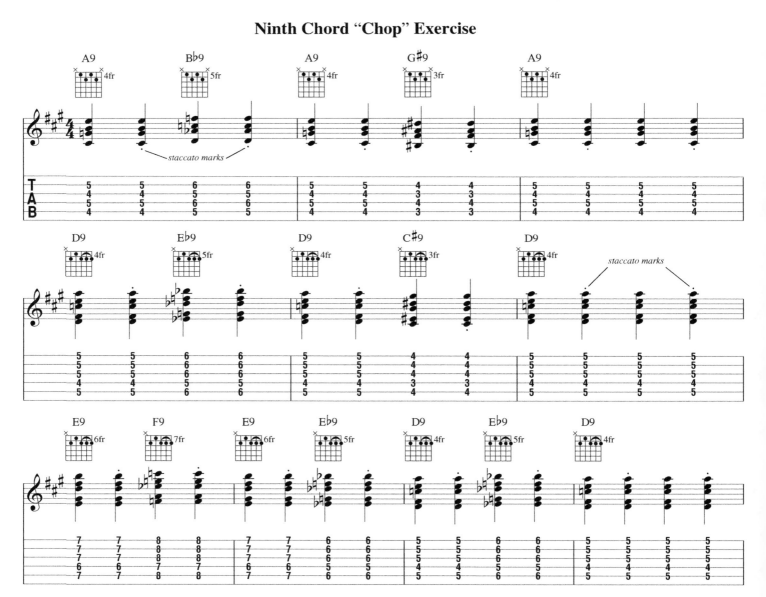

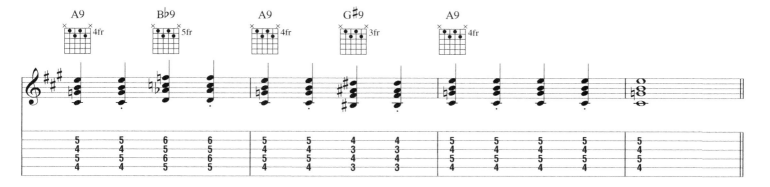

At the end of measures 5 and 8 in the study below, you'll see a quarter note tied to the first part of a triplet (marked by a line above the notes with a "3" in it). This is a bit complex, but if you listen carefully, you'll hear how it goes and shouldn't have any trouble with it.

You will also often see that you play the bass (bottom) note of a chord followed by the rest of it a half-beat later; this is a way to add interest and fill space. You form the whole chord and play the bottom note, then strum through. Don't worry if you hit two strings at first—all of the notes are correct since you are holding the chord, as you saw with the seventh chords in Lesson 6.

If ninth chords are new to you, be careful not to overdo it while practicing them. They can create a strain on the knuckles of your third finger, because it has to bend backwards. Take it slowly and give your fingers time to limber up.

  # NINTH CHORD RHYTHM IN A

TRACK 16   TRACK 17
Full Band   Play-Along

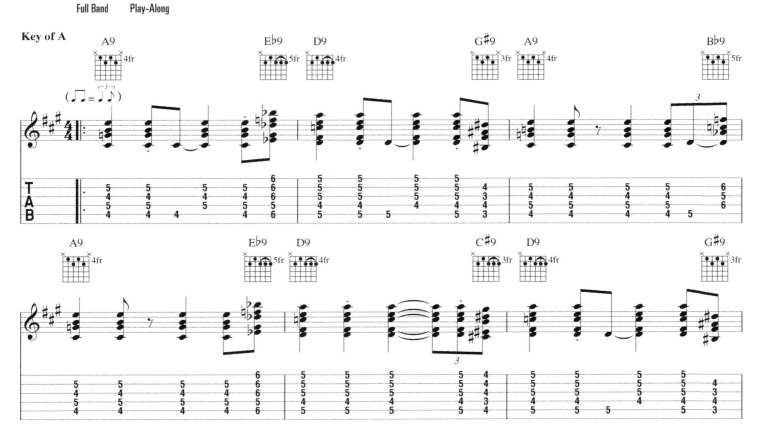

HIGH NINES IN D

In this lesson's study, we'll use the same ninth chord shapes that we learned in Lesson 8, but in a different way.

We'll also use approach chords like in Lesson 8, but we'll add a bit to the progression as well.

Finally, we'll make fairly extensive use of *triplet rhythms*—in this case, *eighth-note triplets*. You'll learn how to get around with these rhythms.

Everything else is fairly straightforward.

THE CHORDS (HARMONY):

Set 1 and 2 Ninth Chords

The chords used in this study are ninth-chord shapes based on the "Ninth Chord Rhythm in A" from Lesson 8. There is a difference though: the function of the different shapes is reversed. The I chord is a 5th-string-root chord used for the IV and V chords in the last study, and the IV and V chords in this tune are the 6th-string-root chords. Together they constitute Set 2 of the I, IV, and V chords discussed in the last chapter, and in Lesson 4 of *Blues You Can Use*.

In Set 1, the I chord has a 6th-string root, and the IV and V chords have 5th-string roots. The root of the IV chord is found on the same fret as the I chord. The root of the V is found two frets up from the IV chord.

In Set 2, the opposite is true, where the I chord is a 5th-string-root chord, and the IV and V chords have 6th-string roots. The root of the IV chord is found two frets down the neck from the I, and, as always, the root of the V chord is two frets above the root of the IV on the same string.

Here are examples of Sets 1 and 2 in the spread style as well as with seventh and ninth chords. Look it over carefully and make sure you understand it. This is a very important aspect of fingerboard layout. If you already have a solid understanding of how the root movement patterns work, you may skip the illustration.

I–IV–V Root Movement Pattern in the Key of D (Sets 1 and 2)

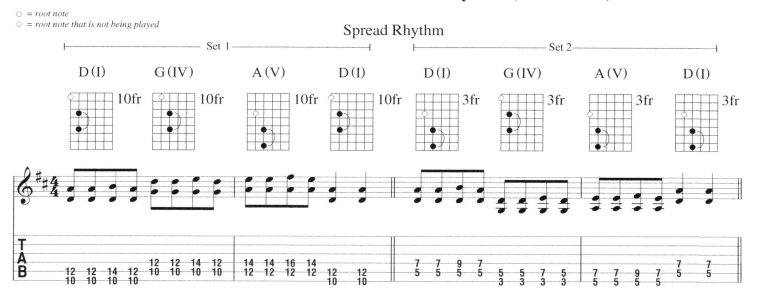

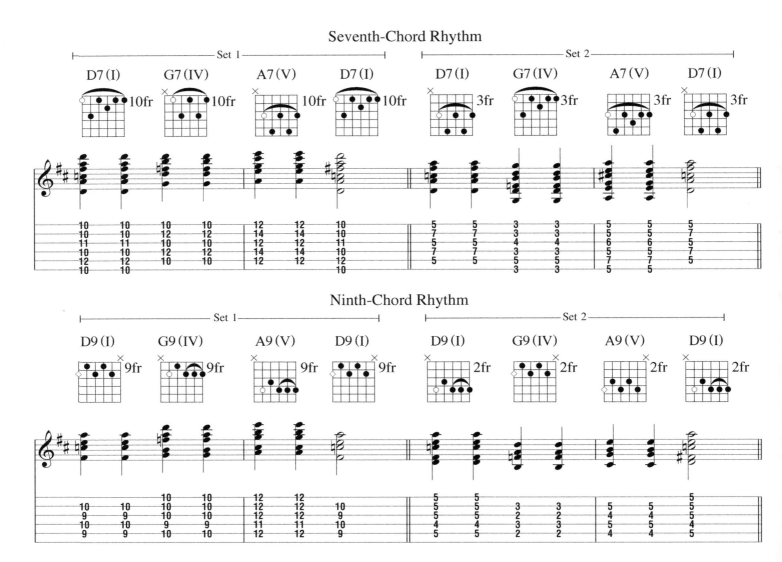

♭II Chord

The progression includes numerous approach chords, marked in the score. There is a ♭II chord (E♭9) in measure 3; it is just there to break up the two-bar stretch of the I chord and doesn't really count as a chord change. You hear it in a slow blues fairly often and, as long as all the rhythm players play it, you can put it in most tunes.

THE STRUMS (RHYTHM AND TECHNIQUE):

Quarter-Note and Eighth-Note-Triplet Combos

"High Nines" has a simple progression, but it is rhythmically complex. There is quite a mix of quarter notes, eighth notes, and eighth-note triplets in the tune. These are what present you with the biggest challenge.

When you mix rhythms, like those in this study, it is easy to confuse them at first. For that reason, you have to start out slowly and carefully as you learn them; take the time to get it right the first time. This way you won't have to unlearn the mistakes and relearn it correctly.

The way they work is simple. The tunes are in 4/4 (four-four) time. (That means there are four beats per measure [bar] and a quarter note gets one full beat, so there are four quarter notes in each measure.)

Just as you'd expect with fractions, there are two eighth notes in the space of one quarter note, so there are eight eighth notes per measure. Finally, there are three eighth-note triplets in the space of one quarter note, so there are three eighth-note triplets in a single beat, or 12 per measure. Look at the following chart to see more clearly how that works.

Quarter-Note, Eighth-Note, and Eighth-Note Triplet Rhythms

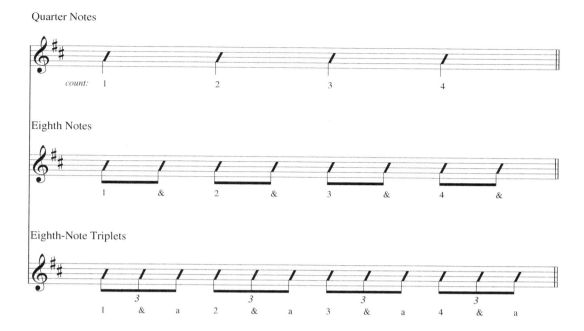

Below is an exercise to help you move between them. Take your time and don't rush. Note that this drill is not based on a blues progression, but is a simple two-chord movement to facilitate the rhythmic work.

Rhythmic Exercise
Quarter Notes, Eighth Notes, and Eighth-Note Triplets

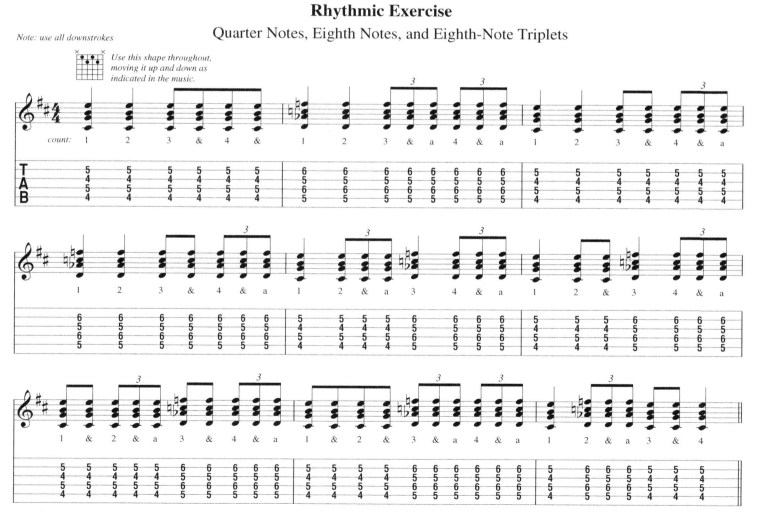

You really want to get these rhythmic elements down, after all, you are studying *rhythm* guitar. Aside from the chords themselves, the accompaniment styles are more characterized by the strumming rhythms than anything else.

Now start working on the study itself:

HIGH NINES IN D

LESSON 10

SIXES AND NINES

Now we'll look at a device commonly used in the blues where you slide between ninth and sixth chords. The chord shape stays the same, making it possible to play smoothly. You'll instantly recognize the sound.

We'll also add some notes to the ninth chords that you know and shave some notes off of other ninth chords, in order to make them easier to play and manipulate.

You'll learn how to put Sets 1 and 2 of the I9–IV9–V9 chords together, and mix and match them. The study is three choruses long, so we can investigate more ways to use the chords.

THE CHORDS (HARMONY):

Chord Fragments

As I mentioned above, the chords used in this study are formed from the basic ninth chords we used in the last two studies. But, in many cases, some notes are omitted and new ones are added to give you a different voicing and slightly different sound. These are often called *partial chords* or *chord fragments*. The fragments used in this study are given below using a 6th-string-root G9 chord, and a 5th-string-root C9 chord as examples. *Remember: the root is not played, but is used to find the chord.* Here they are:

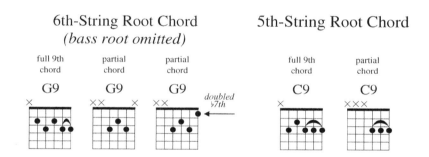

Ninth-to-Sixth Chord Movement

The other new harmonic element is the ninth-to-sixth chord movement mentioned earlier. It is a very straightforward technique: you simply form a partial ninth chord ($\flat$7–9–5 from the bottom up), then move the shape up two frets without changing your fingering. The result is a sixth chord of the same letter name. For example, if you start with a partial G9 chord, as described above, and move it up two frets, you will end up with a G6 chord.

Since you're moving up two frets, there is space for a passing chord between the ninth and the sixth chords. So, if you play the above G9–G6 chord movement, you could put a G$\flat$6 in the space between them. The following diagram shows how to do that.

You can slide the shape up and/or down for an interesting effect.

Here's what it all looks like:

Ninth-to-Sixth Chord Movement
Set 1 and 2 Chords - Key of G

*p = passing chord

"Sixes and Nines" is a three-chorus tune where the first is made up of Set 1 ninth chords, the second of Set 2 chords, and the third is a combination of the two. You want to be able to switch between them with ease.

There are a number of passing chords moving between the ninth and sixth-chord shapes. These are not marked, because at this point you should be able to recognize them.

THE STRUMS (RHYTHM AND TECHNIQUE):

Multi-Stop Slide

The most difficult technique involved in performing this lesson's study is the *multi-stop slide*. *Multi-stop* means fingering (stopping) more than one string at a time. It requires, above all, a very light touch. If you have a light touch in your fretting hand, you will be able to glide along the neck to the target note/chord with ease. If you press too hard, your fingers will get stuck on the frets and it will sound "jerky." Developing the lightness in your fretting hand will make your playing much easier, while improving your tone. It should be obvious that it will also save your hand from fatigue, since you aren't using as much energy to fret a note or chord.

Below is an exercise in sliding from one chord to another of the same shape. Take it very slowly at first. Work for a clean, even, and steady sound. Remember to use the lightest touch you can. It may take some practice, but you will get it eventually, and when you do, you'll see how well it works and how good it feels.

Exercise in Sliding into Chord Shapes

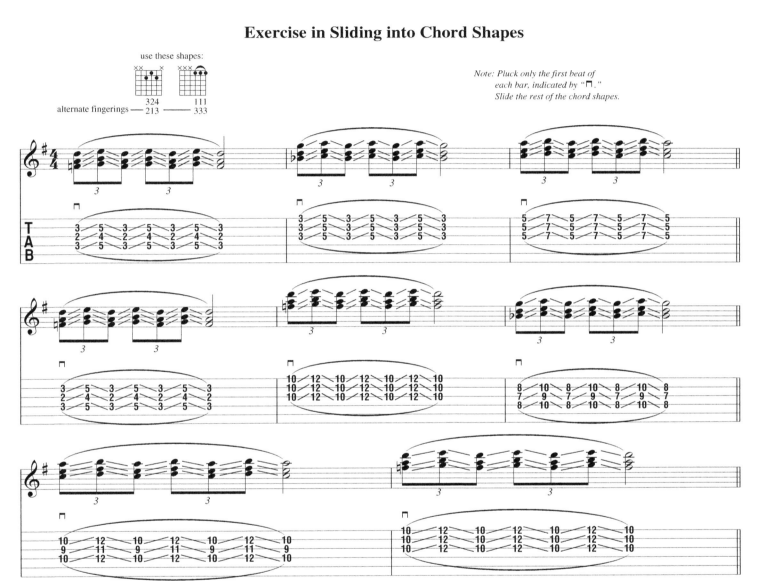

Simplification for Learning

One last thing, before you start working on the study: any time you find these tunes to be too difficult and beyond your current ability, simplify them. This is particularly true with ornaments and articulations. As an example, if you find that you simply cannot play the multi-stop slides discussed above, then leave them out of the study for the time being; learn it without them. Just play the target chords as though there is no slide into them. By all means, do keep working on the multi-stop slide technique through the given exercise and continue to attempt to manage them in the study. But, rather than becoming frustrated with the whole tune, simplify it to learn and practice it. Slowly add a slide or two and eventually you will be able to play it as written—slides and all.

This is a principal that carries over to many aspects of your playing (including your lead playing where you might want to leave out a hammer-on or pull-off, plucking both notes instead, for example). You don't want to give up on the techniques entirely, but you might need to work on them outside of the tune you are learning.

Here's this lesson's rhythm study:

SIXES AND NINES

LESSON 11

NINTH CHORD STUDY IN E♭

In this lesson, we'll continue working with the ninth-to-sixth chord slides, taking them apart and finding new ways to play them. You'll learn a more interesting, and a bit more musical way to play them.

We'll also work more on adding and omitting notes from the chords.

Finally, you'll see how less is often more. This rhythm study is more sparsely arranged than the earlier ones.

THE CHORDS (HARMONY):

The chords in this lesson's study have all been discussed in the last three lessons, so we'll look at the new ninth-chord voicing and how it can be used in an altered arrangement of "Sixes and Nines" (the study from Lesson 10).

Treble String Ninth Chords

The new voicing is a favorite of Buddy Guy, who was the first player I saw use it. It is found on the treble strings (top four), built with the ♭7th in the bass, followed by the 9th and 3rd on the next strings up with the root on the top string. It's a bit tricky to finger at first, but, as is true with all of the chords and techniques, if you practice diligently, you'll get it. Here's what it looks like:

Treble String Ninth Chord

○ = root note

I put it with the chords in "Sixes and Nines" with some changes and simplifications, because it is easier to form when you are already fingering the chords in the tune. Play the following arrangement to see how that works.

Sixes and Nines
(simplified)

THE STRUMS (RHYTHM AND TECHNIQUE):

Elongated Ninth-to-Sixth Chord Slides

While the rhythm study in this lesson makes use of multi-stop slides you learned in the last lesson, they are performed differently. Instead of sliding the whole shape, slide one or two notes, and while still holding the shape, pluck the remaining notes. After that, we continue to hold the whole shape, and slide it back down to the original position. This breaks up the slide figure and creates a more interesting chordal pattern.

When you play an elongated figure like this, without strumming all of the notes at once, the notes first strummed may fade out. If this happens, don't worry. It will still sound good because the listener will remember the sound of the whole chord.

That all sounds more complicated than it really is, so look at the exercise below to see how it works on the guitar fingerboard:

Advanced Exercise in Sliding into Chord Shapes

Use these chord shapes:

Ninth-to-Sixth Chord

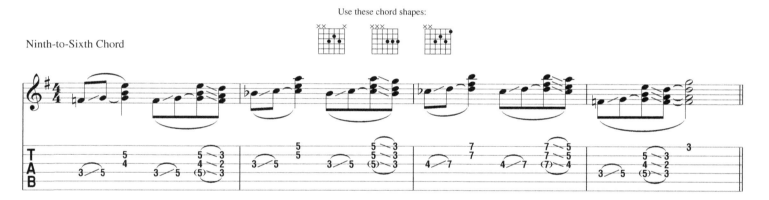

Ninth-to-Sixth Chord
with Passing Chords

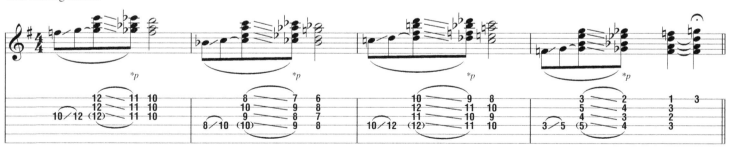

*p = passing chord

Now that you have an idea how the new multi-stop-sliding technique works, start working on the study.

NINTH CHORD STUDY IN E♭

TRACK 22
Full Band

TRACK 23
Play-Along

G MINOR BLUES

Now we are going to turn our attention back to the beautiful, melodic, and often moody *minor-blues* style. You will learn how to make dominant chord shapes minor.

This lesson's study and the next are slow-blues tunes, which makes for a very expressive song. It also allows you to more easily master the chords and progressions.

THE CHORDS (HARMONY):

You have already learned how to build 5th- and 6th-string-root dominant seventh chords in Lesson 6. You saw how we simply add the ♭7th to a major triad. Making minor chords works in the same way, except we add a ♭7th to a *minor triad*.

Adding the ♭7th to a Minor Triad to Make Minor Seventh Chords

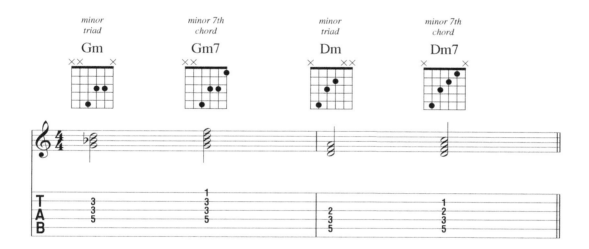

Building Minor Seventh Chords

There is an easier way to make minor seventh chords: take a dominant seventh chord and *flat the 3rd* to make it minor. It's quite simple really.

The third of the 6th-string-root dominant seventh chords we have been using is found on the third string. All you have to do to make the chord minor is flat the 3rd, or move it down one fret. For example, locate the 3rd of the G7 chord on the 3rd string, 4th fret, lower it one fret and you will have the minor 3rd.

You use a similar process to make a 5th-string-root minor seventh chord. The 3rd of the dominant seventh chord is found on the 2nd string. Flat it, and you have a minor seventh chord. Using a C7 chord as an example, the 3rd is found at the 5th fret. Flatting it will result in a minor 3rd at the 4th fret. The following example illustrates this.

Making Dominant Seventh Chords Minor

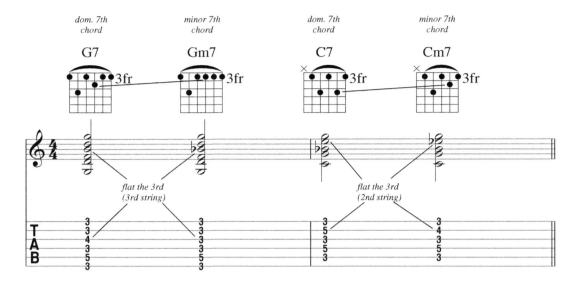

Dominant V Chord in Minor Keys

Again, when we use the roman numerals I, IV, and V for the primary chords of the key, we make them lowercase to indicate that they are minor. So they would be i, iv, and v chords.

In a pure minor blues key, the v chord is minor, and in the 9th measure where the V chord usually is found, there is a minor seventh chord (Dm7). But, in the turnaround, the final V chord is a dominant chord. It is in fact a D7♯9 chord. This use of a dominant chord makes a stronger movement to the i chord. While a Dm7 chord moves well to a Gm7 chord, a D7 moves there with more of a sense of resolution, because the dominant seventh chord has more tension that is released by resolving to the i chord. A minor seventh chord doesn't feel like it has to go anywhere in particular.

While a dominant seventh V chord will work well in a minor blues progression, a ninth chord has to be altered to fit the key. The 9th of the chord either has to be sharped (raised one fret), or flatted (lowered one fret). The following example illustrates how to alter it:

Altering the Ninth of a Dominant Chord (♯9 and ♭9)

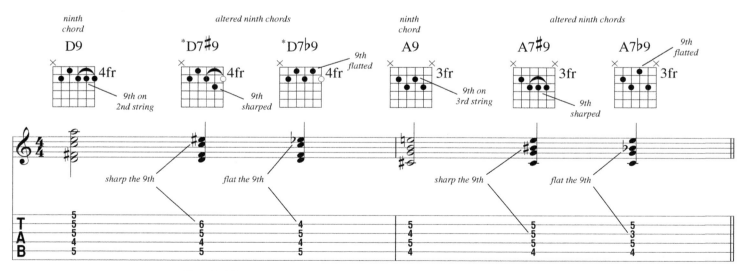

*Note: the 5th (top note) of this chord voicing is usually omitted in the altered 9th form of the chords for ease of fingering. It is shown in the diagrams as an open circle.

THE STRUMS (RHYTHM AND TECHNIQUE):

Dotted-Sixteenth-Note Rhythms

The strumming in this study is pretty straightforward. The only new element is the dotted-eighth, sixteenth-note combination. This is what gives the tune its syncopated feel.

As you saw in Lesson 7, in 4/4 time, sixteenth notes divide the beat into four even sub-beats. An eighth note is equal to two sixteenth notes, just as it is with any other type of fraction. When you dot a note (place a dot right after it in the score), you add half the value of the note. So, a dotted-eighth note is equal to three sixteenth notes. If you put that together with one sixteenth note, you will have one full beat.

There are other eighth, sixteenth-note combinations in the tune. They are all given in the following exercise. Work through it slowly and be sure to count at first.

Eighth-Note/Sixteenth-Note Combination Exercise

Note: use downstrokes except where indicated by an upstroke symbol - "V"

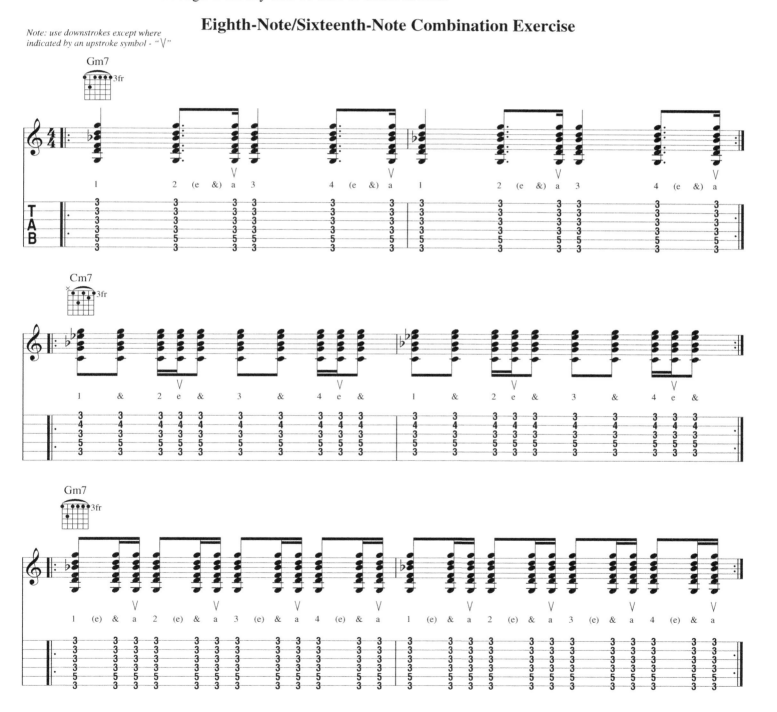

Notice the tied notes in measure 12 of the following study. Look carefully at the strumming marks in the score and listen closely to the recording to see how to play them.

G MINOR BLUES

Note: Use downstrokes except where
indicated by an upstroke symbol - "∨"

Key of G minor

LESSON 13

D MINOR BLUES

We are going to further explore the expressive moods of the minor blues style in this lesson's study. This time, we will be using Set 2 of the i, iv, and v minor seventh chords. You'll see how they correspond to Set 2 of the dominant seventh chords, the only difference is that they are minor.

Also, instead of simply strumming through the chords, we will *arpeggiate* them (play one note at a time). In doing so, you will set out on the road to playing widely varied, interesting, and more professional sounding accompaniment patterns on the guitar.

THE CHORDS (HARMONY):

Set 1 and 2 Minor Seventh Chords

As I mentioned above, in this study, we use the i, iv, and v chords from Set 2 of the root-movement patterns. You will recall that the i chord is a 5th-string-root chord in Set 2, and the iv and v chords have their roots on the 6th string.

You saw a complete list of the I, IV, and V dominant chords from both Sets 1 and 2 in Lesson 9, including those from the spread, seventh chord and ninth chord rhythms. Now, we will look at the minor chord equivalent. As you look at the following chords, keep in mind the root-movement pattern which doesn't change with the types of chords, whether they are dominant or minor, ninth, or simple triads; the root stays the same—it is crucial that you understand that. If you are unsure, go back and study the roots of the chords for similarities between the types and see how they move from one to another.

Here are Sets 1 and 2 of the minor seventh chords:

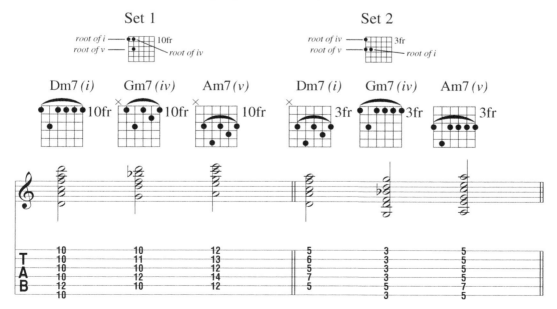

Sets 1 and 2 of i, iv, v Minor Seventh Chords
(Key of D Minor)

Minor Ninth Chords

In this study, we also make use of a new chord: *the minor ninth*. It is the same as a dominant ninth chord, in that it contains a minor seventh chord with the addition of the 9th. You can also build a minor ninth chord by starting with flatting the 3rd of a dominant ninth chord to make it minor. The following diagram illustrates both ways of building a minor ninth chord:

Creating Minor Ninth Chords

Method 1: Adding 9th to Minor Seventh Chords

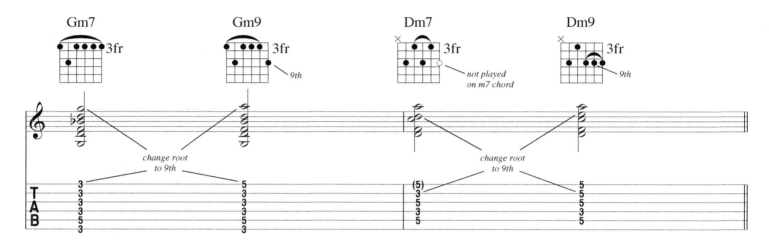

Method 2: Making Dominant Ninth Chords Minor

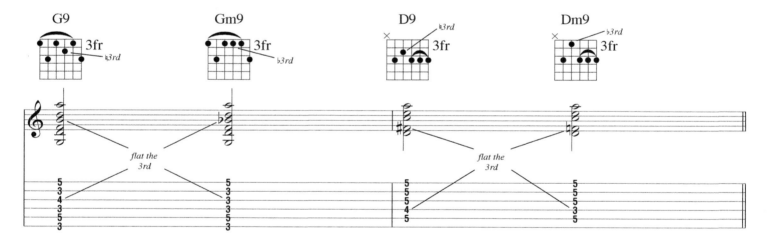

THE STRUMS (RHYTHM AND TECHNIQUE):

Arpeggios

The chording in this study makes use of what are called *arpeggios* (chords played one note at a time). That is, instead of strumming through the whole chord, you pluck each note individually, up or down the chord. You end up with the entire chord by the time you are done arpeggiating it, but it is spread out over time a bit.

Arpeggios make for a more complex and interesting rhythm accompaniment. You hear it especially in slower tunes, in large part, because it is somewhat difficult to do in up-tempo tunes. The style lends itself well to slower, flowing rhythms.

The left hand (fretting) technique is fairly simple—all you do is hold the chord while you pluck the notes. The right hand (picking) is a bit more involved. You need to develop accurate picking and the ability to change direction quickly and smoothly. It's not too difficult, though—it just takes a little practice.

Here is an exercise to help you get started. It is in the key of D minor—the same key as this lesson's study. The chords are straightforward enough. In addition to an Am7 for the v chord, there is an A7 chord in the next measure for a dominant V chord that provides stronger resolution to the i chord (Dm7). Also, the final i chord is a Dm9, which you saw in the "Chords" section of this lesson.

Work through the exercise slowly at first, striving for an even, steady, and clean sound.

Exercise in Arpeggiating Chords

Key of D minor

Note: the V chord changes to a dominant chord in this measure.

The study "D Minor Blues," has nearly the same picking figure. You should be ready to learn it now.

D MINOR BLUES

TRACK 26
Full Band

TRACK 27
Play-Along

Key of D minor

LESSON 14

GOT THE DRIVE

Continuing on with the minor blues style, you'll now see how it doesn't have to be expressively flowing and hauntingly moody. In fact, you can cook in a minor blues! With its repeated rhythmic figure, this study proves it.

You'll learn in this lesson how you can have both a minor i chord and a major IV chord in the same key. It gives you a very different sound, almost ambiguous in terms of its modality—is it major or minor?

THE CHORDS (HARMONY):

The chords themselves are not new to us, however, the combination of chords is.

Minor i–IV Substitute

This study makes use of the I–IV substitute you learned in Lesson 4, with a twist—the i chord is minor, while the IV is major. This provides a unique sound and tonality that you hear from such diverse artists as John Lee Hooker in some of his "boogie" tunes, all the way to Carlos Santana, in his very different latin/blues/rock style. There is also a little bit of "Green Onions," by Booker T. & the MG's in there.

Chords Derived from the Dorian Mode

The basis for this is the *Dorian mode* (a type of minor scale often used in jazz). In the Dorian mode, there is a raised 6th scale step, which is the same note as the 3rd of the IV chord. You will recall that the 3rd is the note that determines whether a chord is major or minor, so if that note is raised, the chord is made major.

In most minor keys, the 6th scale degree is flat, so the iv chord is minor. Here's what it looks like:

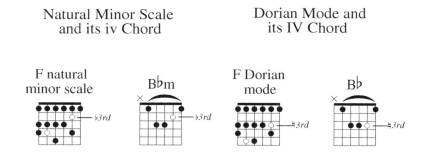

Natural Minor Scale and its iv Chord   Dorian Mode and its IV Chord

Modes are more fully explained in my jazz-blues book, *Jazzin' the Blues* (pp. 9–10), and in most other jazz theory books.

Minor-Major Chords

One last thing: there is an alternate final chord given at the end of the tune. The first final chord given is an Fm9 chord—a voicing we have already seen and used—but in case you are interested in a little more exotic and somewhat dissonant chord, I have included an Fm(maj9) chord—called an F minor-major nine. It is called that because it is a minor triad with a major 7th, replacing the ♭7th of the Fm9 chord. On top of both chords is the 9th. Try it out—you may like it, though it is a bit unsettling.

THE STRUMS (RHYTHM AND TECHNIQUE):

Use of Thumb in Chords

This study employs chord shapes and movements that pretty much require the use of your thumb for the chord's bass notes. Doing so frees up your fingers to make the chord changes with ease. It's not as though you can't use a barre, but it is more awkward.

If you are not used to using your thumb to form chords, take your time and find a comfortable position that works. Try angling your thumb and fretting the bottom string a bit to the side of it—on the finger side. Be careful not to strain it. I find it easiest to fret the string at the knuckle and slightly on the inside of the thumb, but you may find a different position that works better. Just experiment and pay attention to how it feels. Keep your shoulder and elbow relaxed and loose.

Here is a little exercise that will help get you started:

Exercise in Using Thumb to Form Chords

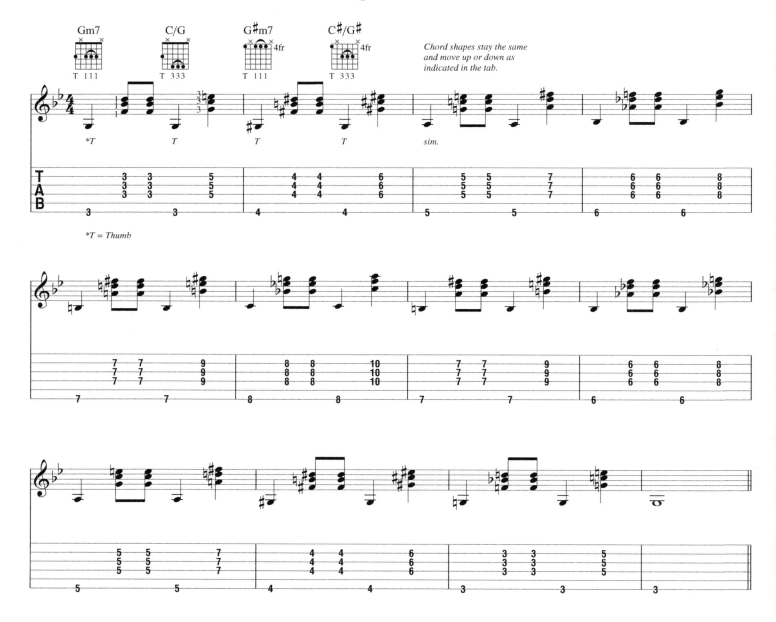

Now start working on the study:

  # GOT THE DRIVE

TRACK 28
Full Band

TRACK 29
Play-Along

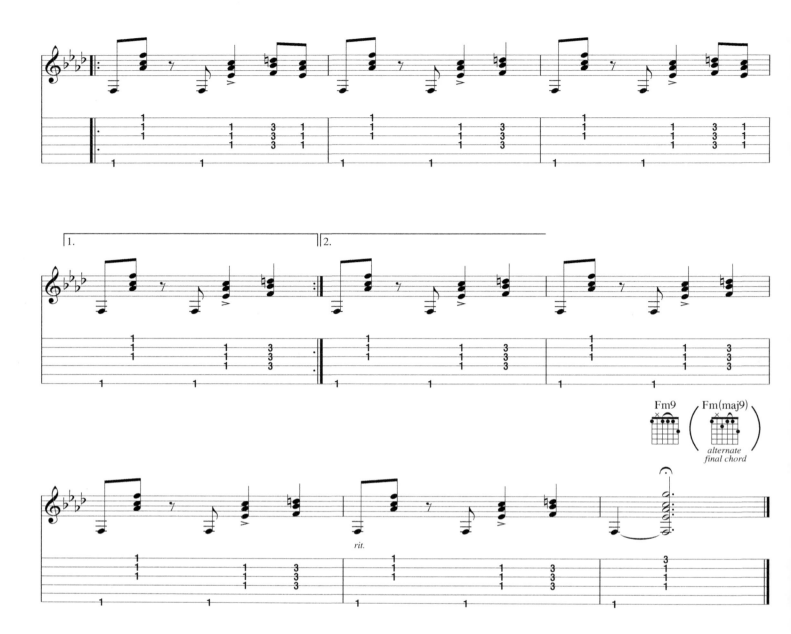

LESSON 15

PASSING CHORD RHYTHM IN A

The chord progression of this rhythm study is taken from *Blues You Can Use*, Lesson 14, "Alternate Progression #1—key of A." It's a 12-bar blues progression, like all of the others in this book, with some interesting chord substitutions.

Rhythmically, it is very austere—an example of the "less is more" school of thought. For most of the tune, there are only two strums per bar, with an occasional single-note lead-in. There are lots of new and familiar chord voicings and even some new chord types.

While it's not really a jazz piece, these are jazz chords. By the time you are through with this study, you'll be able to play jazz-style blues with the best of them.

THE CHORDS (HARMONY):

There are quite a few more chords in this study than in any of the others we have seen so far.

Thirteenth Chords

The tune starts off with a chord type we haven't seen in this book yet: an A13. *Thirteenth chords* technically contain all seven notes of the scale. I say "technically," because there are only six strings on the guitar, so you know that something has to give. In fact, in the case of the first chord, the 9th and 11th of the chord are omitted. Thirteenth chords give you a fuller sound, and like ninth chords, are more complex and sophisticated sounding. Theoretically, they are interchangeable with any other dominant chord (sevenths and ninths, etc.), but as always, your ear is the final judge as to whether it is appropriate or not.

Thirteenth chords also appear in the turnaround, but they are "leaner" voicings (compared to the A13 chord), omitting the 5th and the doubled root as well.

Some musicians feel that because of the missing 9th, they are not really thirteenth chords; most think they are. If you look carefully, you'll notice that the 13th of the chord is the same as the 6th. You'll also notice that the 13th is one fret below the ♭7th of the chord. You will often hear rhythm parts alternate between the two chords.

There is an A13 chord at the end of the tune, which does contain the 9th, so you can compare the three voicings and hear the difference yourself.

Here's what they all look like:

Thirteenth Chords

6th-String Root Voicings

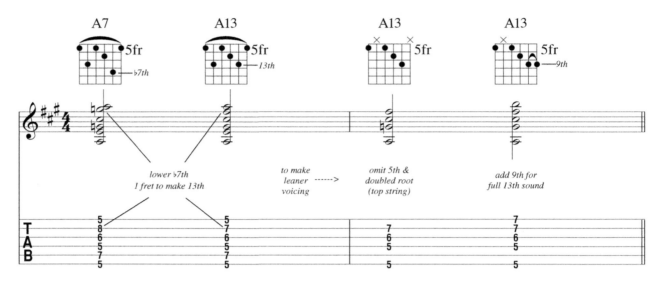

5th-String Root Voicings
(not used in current study)

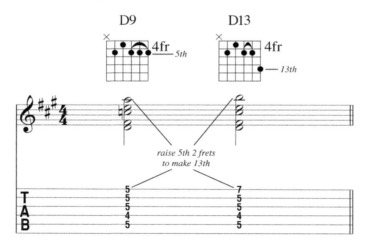

Seventh Sharp Nine Chords

There are three other new chords in the tune: two voicings of an A7♯9 (seven, sharp nine) chord and a diminished seventh chord.

The A7♯9 chords are placed where you would expect some kind of a dominant chord (which they are). You saw in Lesson 12 how to make a sharp nine chord, so here are the two new voicings:

Dominant Seven Sharp Nine Chords

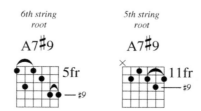

Diminished Seventh Chords

The diminished seventh chord is made up entirely of minor thirds. Because they split the octave evenly, they occur every three frets and any note of the chord can be the root. These are more fully explained on pages 21–22 of *Blues You Can Use Guitar Chords*. For our purposes, you only need to remember this: *diminished chords repeat every three frets and any note can be the root.* Here are two voicings cycled up the neck by minor thirds:

Diminished Seventh Chords (°7)

(any of these chords can be either A°7, C°7, E♭°7, or G♭°7/F♯°7)

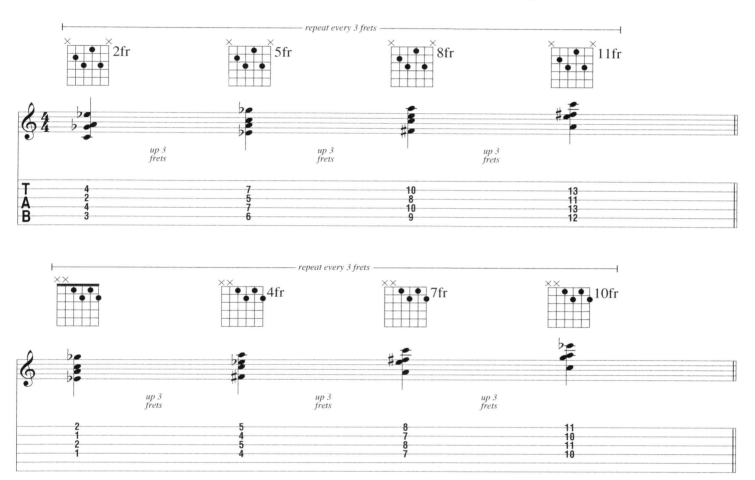

THE STRUMS (RHYTHM AND TECHNIQUE):

Simplification for Easier Learning

The techniques used in this lesson's study are ones we have already used that don't need repeating. There is one technique that is worth discussing—*simplification*. That is, taking a complicated and difficult tune and simplifying it into something that can be more easily performed. The trick is to maintain the integrity of the rhythm. It will be changed—that's unavoidable—but you still want it to be recognizable. You can accomplish that by omitting small things a bit at a time.

Using this lesson's study and the one from Lesson 10 as examples, let's look at how you might make them a bit easier to play.

"Sixes and Nines," the study in Lesson 10, is pretty straightforward, but the multi-stop slides are tricky to play at first. The obvious way to simplify the study is to remove the slides altogether. It will sound different, but the foundation will be intact.

Here's how that would work:

Sixes and Nines
(simplified)

The current study, "Passing Chord Rhythm in A," lends itself easily to simplification. This time, though, you don't take out chordal slides, but instead, remove single note anticipations. That is, single notes that either move to a note of the next chord, or are a part of it. Again, you simply omit them, or maybe only some of them. Sometimes, you only need to remove one note of a two-note run; you can also leave just one of them in.

Look at the following example for ideas:

Passing Chord Rhythm in A
(simplified)

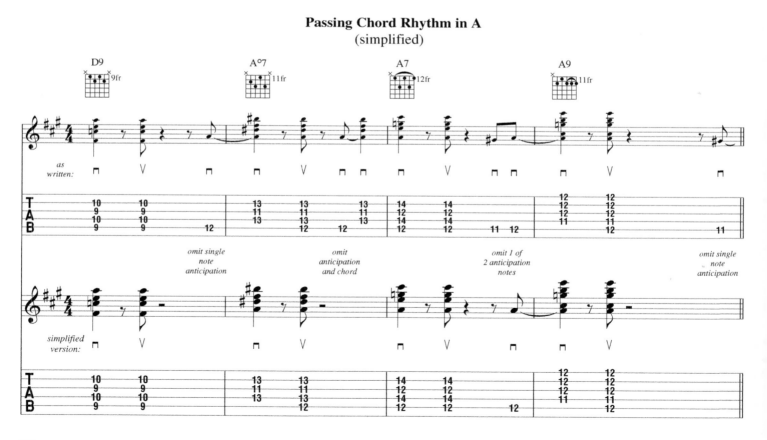

Sometimes it can get tricky choosing which notes or chordal figurations to take out, however, if you keep in mind what the tune should sound like, you should be able to work it out.

TRACK 30
Full Band

TRACK 31
Play-Along

PASSING CHORD RHYTHM IN A

Key of A

TRIPLET STORMY RHYTHM

Continuing with the chordal mix, we are going to explore the use of *secondary chords* in a 12-bar blues progression. These are chords of the key other than the *primary* I, IV, and V chords. In this and most cases, they are minor seventh chords, allowing you to learn more ways to use them.

We will also break down the rhythm into its sub-beat components—eighth-note triplets. You'll see how to make use of the triplet feel in choosing your strumming patterns.

THE CHORDS (HARMONY):

Secondary Chords

As I stated above, this study makes fairly extensive use of secondary chords. They are the ii, iii, vi, and ♭VII chords, in a blues key. We will look at the ii and iii chords in "Triplet Stormy Rhythm."

Very briefly, a dominant blues key has seven chords in it. They are as follows (the actual letter names are given in the key of G—the key of this lesson's study):

Chord	Quality (chord type)	Function in Key	Key of G
I	dominant seventh	primary chord	G7
ii	minor seventh	secondary chord	Am7
iii	minor seventh	secondary chord	Bm7
IV	dominant seventh	primary chord	C7
V	dominant seventh	primary chord	D7
vi	minor seventh	secondary chord	Em7
♭VII	dominant seventh	secondary chord	F7

Here they are using both 6th- and 5th-string-root chords:

Primary and Secondary Chords in Blues (Dominant) Key

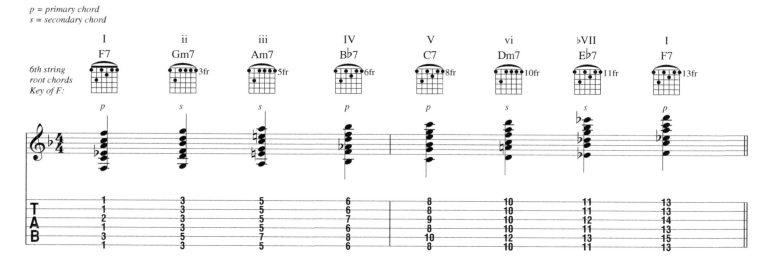

74

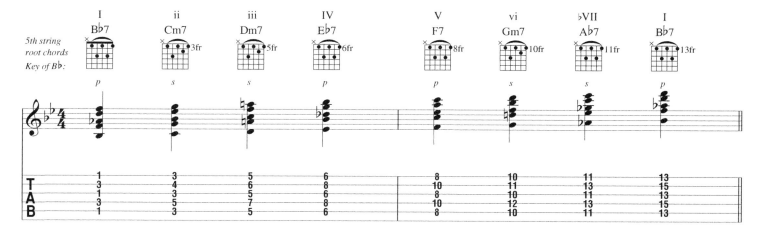

For more information on secondary chords, go to Lesson 18 of *Blues You Can Use*, and the appendix of *Blues You Can Use Guitar Chords*. They both offer fuller discussions.

The progression of this tune has a number of substitute chords: there is a diminished seventh passing chord (G°7) in measure 6, moving between the IV (C7) and I (G7) chords, like the A°7 we saw one in the last lesson. This time it cycles up three frets as you saw in diagram 3 of Lesson 15. Also, in the turn-around you will find a C#°7 chord, which is a passing chord moving between the I and IV chords as well.

THE STRUMS (RHYTHM AND TECHNIQUE):

Triplet Strumming

The strumming for this tune is based on the triplet subdivision of the beat. This means that for each of the four beats in a measure, there are three sub-beats. You count it like this:

1 - & - a, 2 - & - a, 3 - & - a, 4 - & - a

We use that rhythmic pattern to decide where in the beat to place a strum. You might play only the first and third triplets, or all three in a beat—you pick and choose. You have to internalize the triplet feel and become very familiar with it in order to do it with ease. Here is an exercise to help you to get started:

Triplet Feel Strumming Exercise

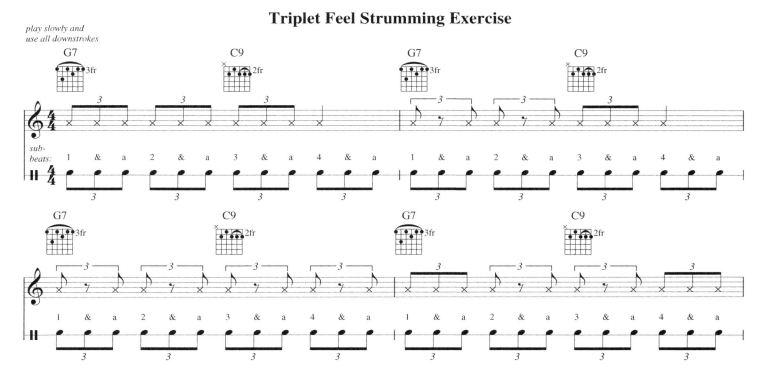

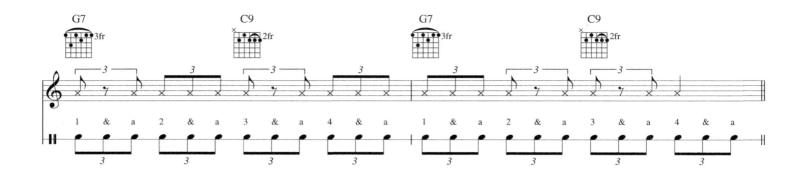

The study has the triplets marked in the score like the above exercise, but here the music is written in 12/8 meter. The tune is still counted in 4/4 time (1, 2, 3, 4).

TRACK 32   TRACK 33
Full Band   Play-Along

TRIPLET STORMY RHYTHM

LESSON 17

JUMP BLUES IN A♭

In this lesson, we will find ourselves on the other side of the beat—the *upbeat*. You will see how a jump-blues rhythm gives a tune an incredible drive, or strong forward motion.

Using chords you have already learned, you will develop a stronger sense of time and a well-controlled strumming technique.

THE CHORDS (HARMONY):

The chords used in this study are not new, and neither is the progression. It is a two-chorus tune, with the first using a combination of dominant seventh and ninth chords, all from Set 1 of the root-movement patterns. The second chorus uses Set 2 chords, again combining seventh and ninth chords.

Interchanging Dominant Chords

How you mix and match sevenths and ninths, or even thirteenths and altered ninth chords, is a musical choice you make based on your personal sensibilities. What sounds good to you may not be the optimal choice for another player. As long as you don't have a note in the chord that clashes with the melody, bass, or horn line, and you stay within the theoretical boundaries of chord choice and interchange, your rhythm part will sound all right. As is always true in these cases, the rest is up to your ear.

You have to experiment to find out what you like and what you don't. For example, while an A13 chord should be interchangeable with an A7 chord, it may not be appropriate for the tune.

To help you hear the differences between the chords, I have provided you with a few examples. The chords given are all in A♭—the key of this lesson's study. You are given multiple A♭ dominant (I) chords that move to a D♭9 (IV) chord. Once you have played through the examples, try making up your own chord movements. Listen closely and see which ones you like and which ones you don't. Remember, just because they are theoretically correct, it doesn't necessarily follow that you will like them all. Don't forget to change the IV chord as well, choosing sevenths and thirteenths to replace the D♭9 chord.

Interchanging Dominant Chords in A♭
Various I Chords (A♭) to IV (D♭9)

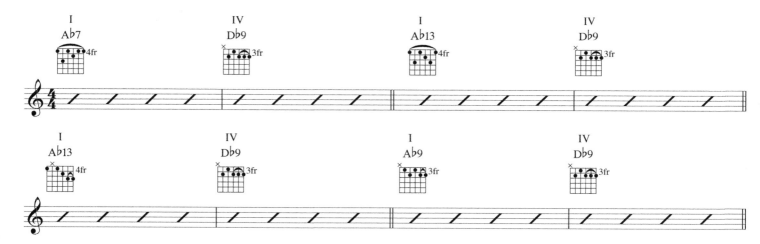

When you have learned "Jump Blues in A♭," we'll try changing some of the chords. Begin by replacing the A♭7 chords with A♭13 in the first chorus, and the D♭7 with D♭13 in the second chorus.

Here are those chords:

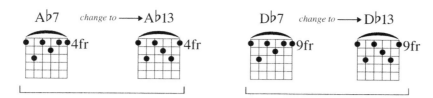

THE STRUMS (RHYTHM AND TECHNIQUE):

Syncopation

The strumming is where this study differs from anything we have looked at so far. Almost all of the strums are played on the upbeat (the & of the beat). Written out, one measure of the beat looks like this:

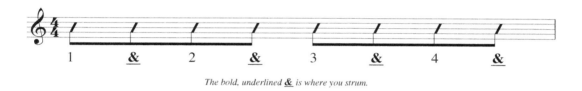

The bold, underlined __&__ is where you strum.

Because it is on the upbeat, you use an upstroke as you strum the chord. There are a few strums on the downbeat, as you can see in the first full measure, that are played with a downstroke. The rhythmic feel is upbeat, syncopated, and drives forward. The reason for this is that you are pushing the beat and chord changes, anticipating the downbeat, as you saw in the spread rhythm of Lesson 3.

The jump-blues rhythm is very simple—almost deceptively so—but it is very easy to lose the upbeat and end up strumming on the downbeat. For that reason, I recommend practicing this with a metronome. Have the metronome on beat 1, 2, 3, and 4, and play on the "&" of each beat.

If you find yourself having any kind of difficulty in playing it, try staying on a single chord for a stretch and eventually move to the next without regard for the actual duration of the chords in the progression. This way, you can focus on the strum without worrying about what chord comes next. It will eventually come, and then you can focus on the chord changes.

JUMP BLUES IN A♭

LESSON 18

ROCKIN' BOOGIE IN A

Now we'll rock out a bit with this lesson's boogie in A. You'll learn how to play melodic lines around a common chord shape, giving you a fuller sound. You'll see how to add notes to chords and, adding them to the chord tones themselves, create new and different types of rhythm guitar parts. And finally, you'll learn how to rock out on the blues!

THE CHORDS (HARMONY):

The chords used in "Rockin' Boogie" are common and should already be familiar to you; if they aren't, don't worry. We'll look closely at where they come from and how they work.

Major Chord Shapes

The basic shape used is from the open A major chord, played in the first position (you surely know that one). We use it for the I chord, since we are in the key of A. For the IV and V chords, we use the same shape, only played further up the neck. The 5th-string roots of the IV (D) and V (E) chord shapes are given in the diagram, though they are not played (you need to see them to find the chords). The chord shapes themselves are all played on the 2nd, 3rd, and 4th strings, and are all fretted with the first finger.

Rhythm Riffs

Once we have selected the chord shape to use, we add non-chord tones to give us enough notes to make melodic lines. Then, while holding the chord shape, you play the little melodic riffs; they should be very short melodic fragments. You have to keep in mind that you are playing an accompaniment to someone else's solo or vocal part. You don't want to interfere with what the soloist is doing or step on their toes.

To show you what I mean, here are examples of rhythm riffs over the I, IV, and V chords in the key of A, that use the A chord shape. The fingerings are determined by the one-finger-per-fret technique. They are given in the following diagram:

Playing Melodically Off of an A Shape

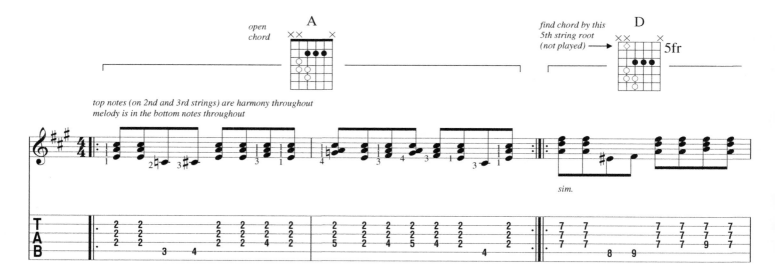

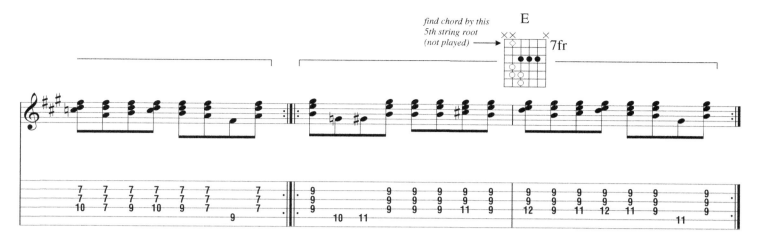

There is another chord shape used, based on the open E chord. It is not as recognizable, because we only play the bottom three strings. It is used for the V chord in measure 12. The riff is pretty much the same as the one used throughout the rest of the tune. Here's how that looks:

Playing Melodically Off of an E Shape

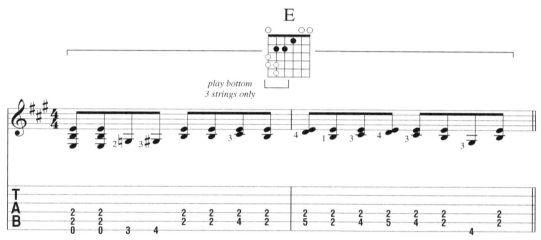

Be sure you understand how all of the above chord/riff rhythms work. They're really very simple.

THE STRUMS (RHYTHM AND TECHNIQUE):

Swing Eighth-Note Strum

This strumming involves swinging the eighth notes throughout the entire tune. You could play it without a swing feel, achieving a Chuck Berry-like, straightforward, driving, steam-engine, rocking feel. But here, we're aiming for a nice bluesy, jazzy feel. The swing is lighter than some we have seen, so don't overdo it; if you do, you'll lose some of the drive.

Once again, you have to tighten up your strumming in this tune in order to avoid hitting strings not included in the rhythm. The biggest challenge is to avoid hitting the top string when using the A shape and the 3rd string when using the E shape. It takes practice, but with time, you will be able to hit only the strings you want.

Rests and Syncopated Pushes

There are some places in the tune where syncopation is involved. In the first two measures, you will notice that there is a *rest* (silence) on beat 4 of measure 1. The rest symbol looks like this: 𝄾. The first two rests are labeled in the score, after that you'll have to find them yourself.

The break created by the rest is followed by a push on the upbeat, which is held over into the downbeat of the 2nd measure. Following that, there is another push held into the next downbeat of measures 2 and 3. That two-measure rhythm is repeated, for the most part, throughout the tune.

This gives the tune the forward motion of Lesson 3's "Spread for Mr. Reed," and several of the tunes that follow. Following along in the score, listen closely to the audio example to hear what it sounds like. You shouldn't have much trouble with it.

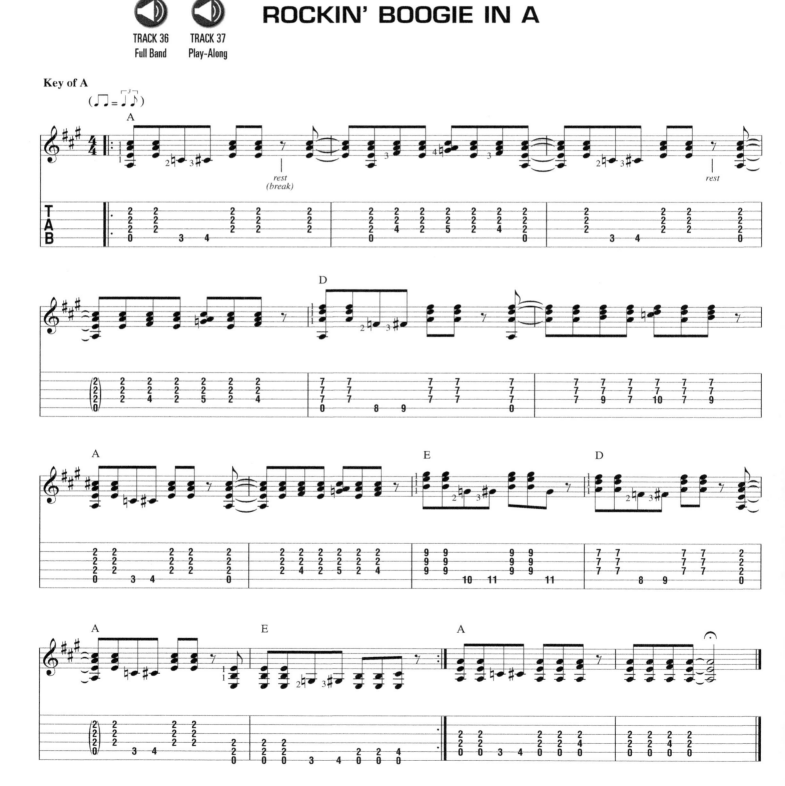

ROCKIN' BOOGIE IN A

TRACK 36
Full Band

TRACK 37
Play-Along

LEAD RHYTHM IN C

In "Minor Triad Blues," you played little lead guitar riffs or fragments of riffs before strumming the chords. You also added little single-note runs in the last study, "Rockin' Boogie in A," playing them off the chord shapes. In this lesson, we'll look at a more extensive use of lead riffs in a rhythm guitar part. The technique is often called *lead rhythm*, for obvious reasons.

You hear this style a lot, but it was probably most widely and famously used by the late, great Texas blues guitarist Stevie Ray Vaughan. Another well-known guitarist who has used this style frequently is Eric Clapton. You can hear him playing lead rhythms along with Jack Bruce and Ginger Baker on any of the Cream albums. Though some forget that they contain some great blues playing, I have always felt you can hear some of Clapton's best blues work on them.

THE CHORDS (HARMONY):

Lead Riffs in Rhythm Part

The chords in this lesson's study have all been introduced in earlier tunes. All of the chords are built on the Set 1 root-movement pattern you saw in Lesson 9, where both Set 1 and Set 2 are fully explained. If you don't remember it, go back and look it over.

The I and IV chords in the body of the tune are 6th-string-root and 5th-string-root seventh chords, respectively. The V chord is a 5th-string-root ninth chord, still derived from the Set 1 root-movement pattern. We are simply mixing dominant chord types—sevenths and ninths—as was discussed in Lessons 8 and 15. Here's how the root-movement pattern is used as a basis for the chords:

Building Chords on Set 1, I–IV–V Root-Movement Pattern

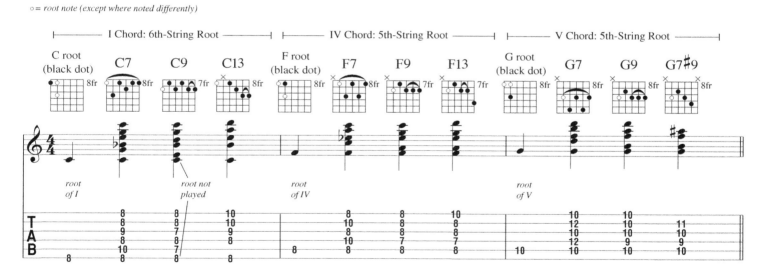

You can use either root-movement pattern as a basis on which to "plug in" any type of dominant chord that your ear tells you sounds good.

Chord and Pentatonic Scale Relationships

The lead guitar riffs for the I chord come from the C minor pentatonic scale found at the 8th fret, in the same position as the C7 chord. The riffs for the IV chord are from the F pentatonic minor scale, also in the 8th position, where the F7 chord is found.

While there aren't any riffs accompanying the V chord (G9), we could use the G pentatonic minor scale found two frets up from the F scale. You can see in the following diagram that the chords and scales are in or near the same positions; that's so that you don't have to move too far along the neck as you change from riff to chord strum.

Here's what the chord/scale relationship looks like:

Minor Pentatonic Scales Matched with Dominant Chords

For a more thorough discussion and full list of chord/scale pairings, see *Blues You Can Use*, pp. 74–75 for minor pentatonic matches, and p. 80 for the major pentatonic pairs.

THE STRUMS (RHYTHM AND TECHNIQUE):

Fret-Hand Position

The biggest challenge in this study is changing from single-note lines (the riffs) to chord strums. Do your best to keep your fretting hand and wrist in the same basic position. If you change that too much, it will be a lot harder to play. Keep your wrist fairly straight and flat when you are playing the chords or riffs. Also, keep your thumb in roughly the same position on the back of the neck. Don't grip the neck like a baseball bat, with your thumb around the top of the fingerboard and the neck flat against your palm. You want to have a little bit of space between your palm and the neck.

Experiment with the above ideas very slowly at first; be patient and remember that it takes a while to develop new techniques.

Rather than give you an exercise to help you work out the technique, I will let the study itself perform that function. As you have done in previous studies, you can focus on one or two measures at a time. Then you can concentrate on developing the lead/rhythm technique without having to think about what chord or riff comes next.

LEAD RHYTHM IN C

TRACK 38
Full Band

TRACK 39
Play-Along

LESSON 20

ROCKIN' BLUES FOR JIMI

Now we'll return to the blues-rock style while continuing the lead-rhythm technique from the last lesson. You'll learn further how to use lead guitar riffs as fills between the chord changes. In this tune, we'll be moving quickly around the fingerboard, so you'll get a good workout in playing licks and forming chords immediately afterward.

This rhythmic feel and style was developed by such greats as Lonnie Mack, Stevie Ray Vaughan, and, of course, Jimi Hendrix, so you'll be in good company.

THE CHORDS (HARMONY):

More Seventh Sharp Nine Chords

The chords in this study were favored by Jimi Hendrix. They include seventh sharp nine chords that were first introduced in Lesson 12 and discussed further in Lesson 15. This chord type is used for the I chord (E7♯9) which gives us quite a bite for the tonic chord. It sort of sets everything on edge right at the first downbeat.

The use of edgier altered ninth chords can really create a biting rhythm part that has great drive. You can use one for the V chord, as well as for the I. It won't work for the IV chord, because the altered 9th of the chord will clash with some notes of the key (most notably the 5th scale degree—the root of the V chord). For the IV, you can use an unaltered, natural ninth chord. The following illustration gives you two sets of I7♯9, IV9, V7♯9 chords, from Sets 1 and 2 of the root-movement patterns.

Altered Ninth Chord Sets (I–IV–V)

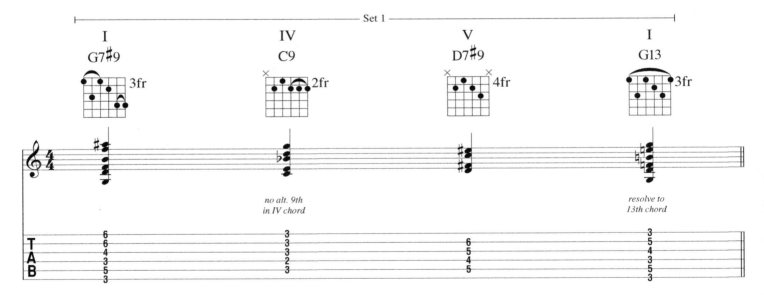

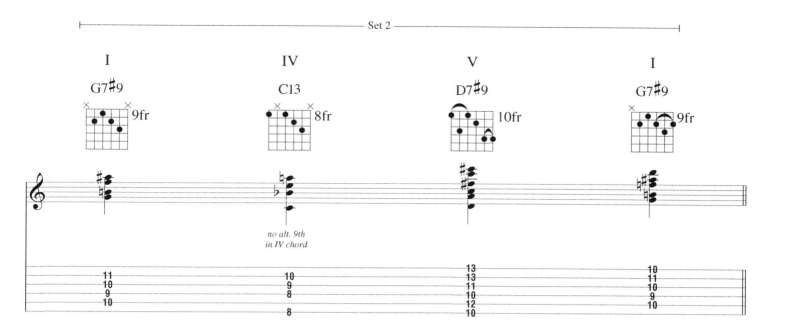

Sharp Ninth to Thirteenth Chord Movement

To give the rhythm a fuller and more solid sound, the low E string is played and allowed to ring while the I chord is sounding. When we move to the IV chord (A13) in the next bar, we include an open A (5th) string and let it ring over that chord.

This is continued throughout the tune, making for a big "wall of sound"—for a single guitar anyway.

The chord shapes themselves are interesting. They contain smaller shapes within them which don't change, but only move up or down the neck by a half step. If you look at the top three notes of the E7#9 (I) chord, you'll see that beginning on the 4th string, 6th fret, they make a straight line that slants toward the top string. Looking at the next chord, an A13 (IV), you'll notice that the top three strings form the same line, but now it begins at the 5th fret—down one half step. The roots move independently of the movement of the above line.

If you look further, you'll see that the movement from the E7#9 chord to the B7 (V) chord in measures 7 through 9 also has the same type of movement of the shape; this time, it is shortened in the B7 chord—the top note is omitted. You could make the V chord a B13, which includes the note on the 2nd string, and end up with the whole three-string shape at the 7th fret.

Knowing that, you can play that shape for the I chord in 6th position, 5th position for the IV, and 7th position for the V chord. The chord names would be: E7#9 (I), A13 (IV), and B13 (V). Try it and you'll hear the I–IV–V changes, even without the root.

You can play only those notes and, as long as you have a bass player giving you the bass notes, you'll still hear the changes as though you played the full chords.

You can also drop the #9 and 13 of the chords and end up with plain seventh chords. Again, you can play them without the roots and still hear the chord changes.

Here's what they all look like:

Two- and Three-String Shapes Moving Through 7th, 7♯9, and 13th Chords

○ = root note

Basic 7th Chords   7♯9 and 13th Combinations

2-string shape moves down 1 fret		*2-string shape moves up 1 fret*		*3-string shape moves down 1 fret*		*3-string shape moves up 1 fret*	
I	IV	I	V	I	IV	I	V
E7	A7	E7	B7	E7♯9	A13	E7♯9	B13

down 1 fret   *up 1 fret*   *down 1 fret*   *down 1 fret*

Note: the roots move independently—not with the static shapes

THE STRUMS (RHYTHM AND TECHNIQUE):

Shapes Common to I–IV–V Chords

When you are playing "Rockin' Blues for Jimi," you often pluck open strings and let them ring through the measure, providing the bass note for the chord. You want to be very aware of them and make sure that you don't accidentally mute them. The key is keeping your fretting fingers away from the ringing open strings. The open strings to be held are marked in the score.

The challenge in this tune is the long shifts from one position to the next as you play a riff and then the following chord. You will probably need to break the tune down into smaller, more manageable chunks as you learn it. Each chunk should consist of a riff and the chord it leads to. For example, one smaller piece would include the opening riff and the E7♯9 chord. You could also include the change to the A13 chord if it isn't too difficult. If it's more than you can manage at first, leave the A13 out until you have worked on the riff and first chord. Practice it over and over until you feel that it's coming, or you just can't stand it any more for that session (I get that way sometimes).

Next you would practice the riff in measure 2 and the E7♯9 chord in measure 3. That shouldn't take as much time as the first chunk you worked on because it is very similar. (Don't spend too much time on what you already know—focus on the things that are difficult for you.) Then, you would move on to the riff in measure 4, and the next A13 chord in measure 5.

Continue in this way until you have practiced all of the smaller segments. Then you can start putting them together. You'll find that you learn the tune faster and better this way because you don't waste time playing through parts that you know well. This allows more time to learn the parts that need work.

Go to the study and start working on it in the above fashion.

ROCKIN' BLUES FOR JIMI

Key of E

DOMINANT RHYTHM IN G

Well, you've made it! This is the last study where I pull out all the stops and let loose with an active rhythm part that can stand on its own as a solo guitar piece. For that reason, I decided not to include a solo of any kind, though it would easily support one. As you work through it, you'll learn how to get around on the chords using devices we learned in the previous 20 lessons, and some new ones.

You could play this tune for your friends, or family members who are always asking you to show them what you have been working on all these months and years. It has enough harmonic and melodic interest, so you don't need a band or backing tracks to fill out the song.

THE CHORDS (HARMONY):

Partial Seventh and Ninth Chord Voicings

There are some new chord voicings in this study, but most of them are derived from the bigger, more basic ones you already know.

The first new chord is also the first chord in the tune. It is a simple 6th-string-root seventh chord—G7 in this case, but there are no doubled notes. Instead, it is a four-note chord with a muted 5th string.

In the fifth measure, there is a C9 chord with the root omitted. You probably would recognize it as the 5th-string-root ninth chord—without the root! You should recall that the root, 5th, or both may be omitted from seventh or ninth chords. The 3rd, ♭7th, and in the case of a ninth chord, the 9th, are essential notes.

Here are the above chords with the larger forms they come from:

Smaller Chords from Larger Forms

Often, you will find that smaller chords are more easily fingered and allow for more agile playing.

In the 6th measure, there is a new ninth chord shape: the first C9 shape in the measure. Actually, it is a ninth chord with a sus4. It's quite a mouthful, but it simply means you have a ninth chord with the 3rd raised by a half step. The following illustrates how you change the ninth chord into the ninth sus4 chord used in the study, beginning with the seventh chord as the basis for both.

Morphing a C7 Chord into a C9sus4 (via C9)

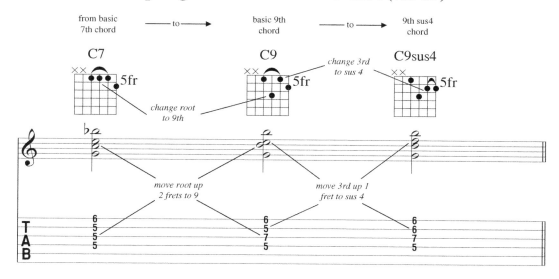

THE STRUMS (RHYTHM AND TECHNIQUE):

Active Melodic Rhythms

In this study, we really take apart the chords and play bits of them to create a very active, almost melodic rhythm. You still finger all or most of the chord, but generally pluck only two or three notes at a time.

In the first measure, you play the chord's bass note and follow it with the ♭7th on the upbeat. Then, while holding the first two notes, you play the ♭3rd and 5th together. Those are followed by a hammer-on to the 3rd and, all the while, you hold down the bass note with your thumb.

Here's an exercise to help you learn this simple technique:

Seventh Chord Hammer-On Exercise

Another technique using the same chord shape as above involves holding the bass note with your thumb while moving your first and second fingers down, then up one fret. This requires a relaxed hand and light touch. You can find examples in measures 3, 4, and 11 of this study. Following is an exercise to help you get the technique down.

Moving Shape Up and Down while Root (Bass Note) Stays Constant

Note: let root ring until next chord change

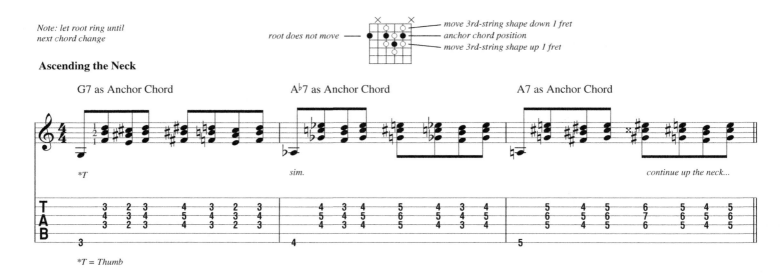

Ascending the Neck

G7 as Anchor Chord   A♭7 as Anchor Chord   A7 as Anchor Chord

*T

sim.

continue up the neck...

T = Thumb

Descending the Neck

A7 as Anchor Chord   A♭7 as Anchor Chord   G7 as Anchor Chord

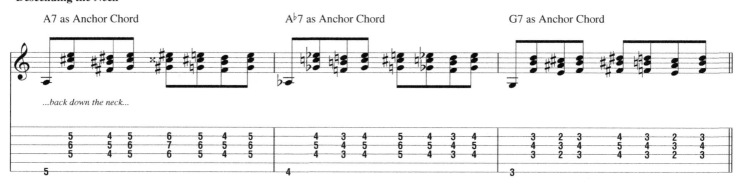

...back down the neck...

Whenever you find yourself facing a difficult lick, chord change, or the like, isolate it like we did above and practice it up and down the neck. It really helps you to nail it. Just make sure that what you isolate and practice is a very short fragment. If there is a longer bit you need to work on in this way, break it into smaller fragments.

All through the study, you need to have tighter, more controlled picking. Take your time with it and work on smaller pieces as we did in the last lesson.

DOMINANT RHYTHM IN G

Key of G

WHERE TO GO FROM HERE

I hope you have gotten a good handle on rhythm playing by studying this book. Now that you have finished this course, you may want to go further. There are some specific things you can do that will help:

First, listen to all kinds of blues recordings. Listen to Albert Collins, Albert King, and of course, B.B. King. Try listening to Freddie King, Robert Cray, Bobby "Blue" Bland, and T-Bone Walker. They all have great rhythm sections with lots of fabulous rhythm guitar parts. Some of them are pretty far down in the mix, so listen closely.

Listen to the piano and organ parts in the recordings. You can get a lot of ideas from them—especially the piano parts.

Play along and try to copy the rhythm players, whatever their instrument. Then, try to find your own part and play to the tune.

Also, learn chord theory (harmony). Study it diligently. Get *Blues You Can Use Guitar Chords*, if you don't already have it, and study it thoroughly. Find yourself a good private teacher or class, and work to expand your harmonic knowledge and add to your stock of chord voicings and progressions. Study some basic jazz chords—they sound great in the blues. We used a lot of them in this book. Learn common chord substitutions. We used some of those in this book as well.

Go to **BluesYouCanUse.com** and **JohnGanapes.com** on the web to see what there is for you there. You will find rhythm studies and more to help you with your playing.

But most of all, play every chance you get. Play with other guitarists at or above your level. Go to jam sessions and play. If you have learned the studies in this book well, they'll really like you at the sessions, because most guitarists don't know much in the way of rhythm guitar. I guarantee you that whoever is running it will want you back, even if all you know is rhythm guitar.

Some people only want to play in their room, all by themselves, and that's okay. But there is nothing like playing with other guitarists to build up your chops. I really would hope that even those of you who feel this way will try it out at least once.

Whatever you do, be sure you are having fun. Remember why you took up the guitar in the first place.